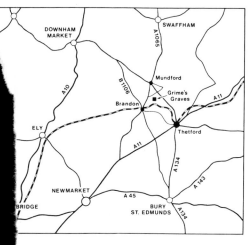

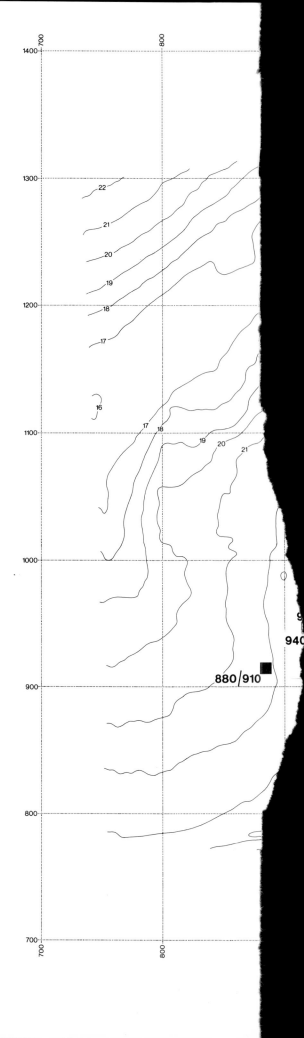

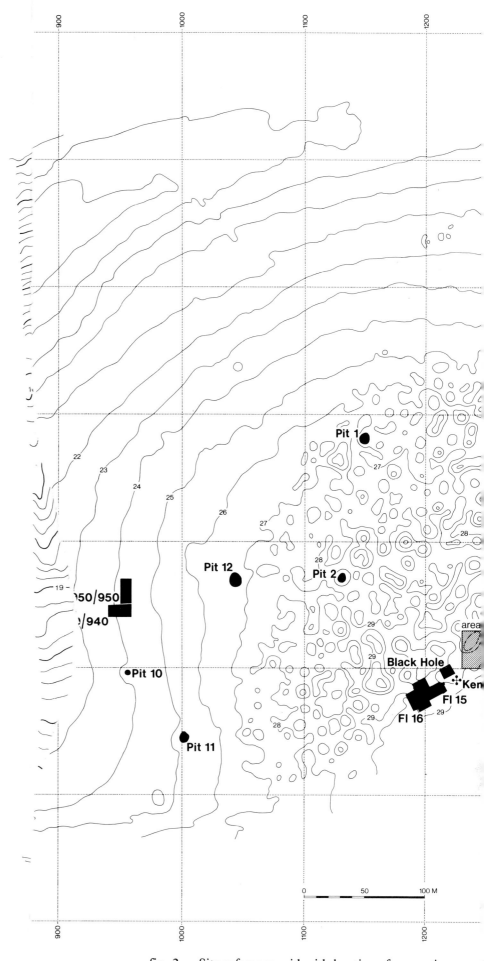

fig. 2   Site reference grid with location of excavations men
For location of excavations in the south-east sector see also

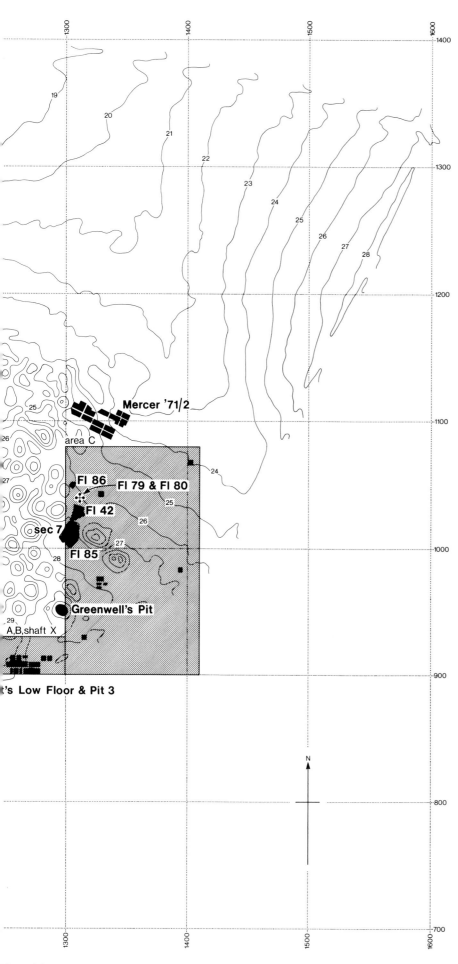

EXCAVATIONS AT
GRIMES GRAVES
NORFOLK
1972–1976

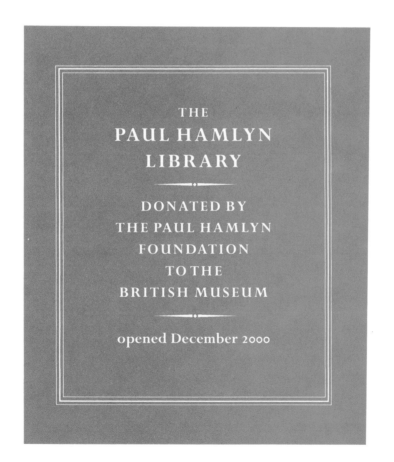

EXCAVATIONS AT
GRIMES GRAVES
NORFOLK
1972–1976

FASCICULE 2

THE NEOLITHIC, BRONZE AGE AND LATER POTTERY

IAN LONGWORTH, ANN ELLISON AND VALERY RIGBY

with a contribution from

IAN FREESTONE

Published for the Trustees of the British Museum
by British Museum Publications Limited

©1988 The Trustees of the British Museum

Published by British Museum Publications Limited
46 Bloomsbury Street, London WC1B 3QQ

British Library Cataloguing in Publication Data
Clutton-Brock, Juliet
Excavations at Grimes Graves, Norfolk,
1972–1976.
Fasc. 2: The Neolithic, Bronze Age and later pottery.
1. Norfolk. Weeting. Neolithic flint mines: Grimes
Graves. Excavation of remains
I. Title   II. Longworth, I.H. (Ian Heaps)
III. Ellison, Ann, 1948–   IV. Rigby,
Valery 936.2′614

ISBN 0-7141-1391-3

Printed in Great Britain by Henry Ling Ltd,
Dorchester, Dorset

Contents

List of Figures

List of Tables

Introduction

The Grimes Graves flint-mining complex lies some six miles north west of Thetford in the county of Norfolk at NGR TL 820900 (fig. 1). For well over a century the site has attracted the attentions of collectors, antiquaries and archaeologists. To Canon Greenwell goes the distinction of having mounted the first recorded archaeological investigation on the site between 1868 and 1870. Between that date and the more recent investigations undertaken by Mercer in 1971-2 (Mercer 1981) and by the British Museum between 1972 and 1976, many explorations were to take place of which the most important were directed by A.E. Peake between 1914 and 1917 (Clarke 1915; Peake 1916, 1917 & 1919) and by A.L. Armstrong from 1920 through to the outbreak of the Second World War, (Armstrong 1921, 1922, 1924a, b, c, 1927, 1932 & 1934). Perhaps because the site was primarily concerned with the extraction of usable flint and had attracted those principally interested in flint implements, the pottery recovered during the earlier investigations has received little attention. Much was left unpublished and some alas no longer remains to be studied. The object of the present volume is to set on record the pottery which now survives from Grimes Graves (excepting that excavated and recently published in Mercer 1981) as part of a series of studies detailing the Museum's recent investigations on the site and ongoing analysis of the materials recovered.

The two main collections derive from excavations undertaken by Armstrong in the twenties and by the British Museum during the research programme carried out on the site between 1972 and 1976, both of which, together with the material excavated by Mercer, are housed in the British Museum. Some pottery also survives in the Castle Museum, Norwich, and we are grateful to our colleagues in that Institution for generously making this material available to us for inclusion.

The pottery has been catalogued in chronological order with a summary of the contexts from which it derives together with a brief general discussion of its significance. Five major points emerge from this analysis:

1   That there is no ceramic evidence for a mining phase before the Late Neolithic.

2   That the main Late Neolithic mining phase associated with the extraction of flint by means of large, deep and often galleried shafts is at present to be seen as the work of those who used Grooved Ware.

3   That while some extraction of flint appears to have continued into the earlier part of the Bronze Age, from then on there is no ceramic evidence to suggest any further extraction on the site.

4   That a considerable Bronze Age settlement using pottery of the Deverel-Rimbury bucket urn type must once have existed in close proximity to the southern and south-eastern margins of the site and that this community was primarily engaged in

pursuing a mixed farming economy with an emphasis on dairy products. (Legge 1981 and forthcoming).

5   That post Bronze Age interest in the site was at best sporadic and that there is no ceramic evidence to suggest any later settlement of any significance in close proximity.

SITE GRID

For the British Museum campaign the site was divided into a grid of 100m squares (fig. 2). Cuttings are referred to by their south-west corners, eastings first.

ACKNOWLEDGEMENTS

I am particularly grateful to Dr Ann Ellison for her collaboration over the analysis of the Bronze Age pottery and to my colleague Valery Rigby for her report on the Late Prehistoric, Roman and and later wares. Dr Ian Freestone kindly agreed to examine a series of sherds by thin-section (see tables 10 & 11) and his report has been incorporated on p.100. I should also like to thank Mr P C Compton for preparing the pottery drawings, Mr S P Crummy for executing the plans, sections and text figures, Mr A Herne for his work on the phasing of the deposits in Shaft X, Miss J Ambers for undertaking the re-calibration of the carbon 14 determinations and Miss Valerie Ives for typing the original text. I would also like to thank Miss Barbara Green and Dr Frances Healy for their unfailing help and willingness to put their own knowledge at our disposal.

I   The Neolithic Pottery

In view of the extent of recorded Neolithic activity and the amount of attention that the site has received over the past century, it is surprising how little Neolithic pottery of any type has been discovered. The majority of sherds belong to the Grooved Ware tradition and this is the only type of pottery to have been recorded in direct association with the actual mining process. A few sherds of Middle Neolithic plain bowl, Peterborough Ware and Beaker complete the list. (For location of contexts see fig. 2).

1   Middle Neolithic Bowl

Eight sherds have been recovered:-

(a)   A rim sherd by Armstrong from Floor 85, and a probable wall sherd from 85A. (For these contexts see p.26).

(b)   Four possible fragments by Mercer from the surface beyond the dump adjoining the 1972 shaft and in the uppermost filling of the 1971 shaft. In both instances the context seems to imply re-deposition (Longworth 1981: 39).

(c)   Rim and wall sherds from Topsoil in the BM's 1974 season in cutting 1325.5/970.5 (*N1* and p.36)

2   Peterborough Ware

Eighteen sherds have been recorded:-

(a)   Fifteen sherds by Armstrong (1934: 386) in Pit 12, Floor C (*N2-9*) (For this context see p.27).

(b)   A single sherd by Mercer from the topmost filling of the 1971 shaft (Longworth 1981: 39).

(c)   A rim and wall sherd (*N10-11*) in the BM's 1973 season in cutting 1263/900.5, the latter in association with a chipping floor. (see p.31).

3   Beaker

Only two certain and four possible Beaker sherds have been recorded from the site:-

(a)   A rusticated Beaker sherd, found on 'the Santon Field' (*N12*).

(b)   A rusticated Beaker sherd, by Peake from Floor 16 (*N14*) (For this context see p.25).

(c)   Four possible plain Beaker sherds by Mercer in a derived context in the topmost fill of the 1971 shaft (Longworth 1981: 39).

4   Grooved Ware

Over 590 sherds of Grooved Ware have been found in varying contexts spread across the site:-

(a)   The Deep Mines
1)   67 sherds by Peake in Pit 1 (Oppenheimer Coll.) (*N21-22, N24, N26 & N28*) (Smith 1915: 208-9).

2)   118 sherds by Peake in Pit 2 (Oppenheimer Coll.) (*N14-20, N23, N25, N27, N29-34*) (ibid., 209-11).

3)   Major portions of two decorated bowls by Mercer from the chalk dump at the base of the 1971 shaft and sherds of plain bowl from Gallery 3. (Longworth 1981: P1-2).

4)   62 sherds plus fragments from one or more plain bowls by Sieveking from one of the SW galleries of Greenwell's Pit and a further 31 sherds and associated fragments, probably from a single bowl, from the basal deposits in the North Western sector of the shaft. (*N35-6*).

(b)   Chipping Floors
1)   A single sherd of plain bowl by Peake from Floor

16 (Norwich Mus. reg. No. 63.948). (For this context see p.25).

2) Two sherds by Mercer in association with a chipping floor to the west of the 1971 shaft.

3) Remains of a plain bowl (*N46*) and thirty three other sherds by Longworth in association with a chipping floor in cuttings 1252.5/905.5, 1255.5/905.5, 1260.5/906.1 and baulks β16, β17 and β40. (see p.31).

(c) Other Mainly derived Contexts

1) 72 sherds by Mercer from Layers I, IA & IB of the filling of the 1971 shaft.

2) Three sherds by Mercer from the surface south of the dump found in the 1971 season.

3) Seventeen sherds by Mercer in the Bronze Age midden layers in the top of the 1972 shaft.

4) 123+ sherds by Longworth from superficial layers in cuttings 1255.5/905.5, 1260.5/906.1, 1260.5/911.1, 1267.5/906.1 and baulks β7, β11, β13 and β18-19. For full list on contexts see table 1 and p.31).

5) Single sherds by Longworth from cuttings 1313/927 and 1325.5/970.5 (table 1 and *ibid*).

6) Thirteen sherds by Longworth from the superficial levels of Shaft X (table 1 and *ibid*).

5 Discussion

(a) Significance for the Site

Middle Neolithic bowl pottery has yet to be recovered from an indisputably stratified context. Its rarity, however, suggests little interest in the area prior to the later Neolithic. Beaker pottery too is notable for its absence, only the single sherd of Rusticated Beaker recovered by Peake from Floor 16 being in context. The Peterborough sherds from Pit 12, Floor C and the single sherd incorporated into the chipping floor in cutting 1263/900.5 during the Museum's excavations indicate some direct involvement of Peterborough Ware users in the exploitation of mined flint but from present evidence it is difficult to gauge either the extent or intensity of that involvement, particularly as sherds of Bronze Age pottery also come from Floor C indicating either later disturbance, or more likely, re-deposition of the Neolithic pottery (see below p.27).

Grooved Ware, however, has been recovered in direct association with the actual mining process in four of the deep mines, and is the only type of pottery to be recorded from that type of context. It is further associated with dumps of chalk rubble derived from the mines and has been recovered on at least two workshop floors in direct association with the manufacture of implements from the mined flint. There can therefore be no doubt that Grooved Ware users represent a major component of those exploiting the flint at Grimes Graves and, on present evidence, they alone have claim to be the miners who created the deep shafts. The distribution of Grooved Ware from the site is, however, with the exception of Pits 1 and 2, heavily biased to the immediate south-eastern fringe of the known deep mining area. The extent to which Grooved Ware users participated in the total exploitation of the site must therefore remain at present an open question.

(b) The Grooved Ware

The Grooved Ware recovered all appears to fall within the Durrington Walls style but significantly represents only one element of the known range of that assemblage. All the sherds so recovered are from bowls and there is no evidence for the presence of the large bucket-shaped storage vessels which form such a predominant element of the style on other sites. The bowls themselves range from the medium coarse and plain to the extremely fine and decorated and probably span the full range of bowl manufacture in the tradition. The plain open bowls are well matched on sites like Fengate, Cambridgeshire (Pryor 1974, figs. 37.10 and 39.14), Mount Pleasant, Dorset (Longworth 1979 P113), Marden, Wiltshire (Longworth 1971 P57-9), N. Carnaby Temple Site 1, Yorkshire (Manby 1974, fig. 17.2, 3 & 5) and Willington, Derbyshire (Manby 1980, fig. 60, 29 & 34), where however they form only one component of the assemblage recovered. The two bowls with incised all-over internal decoration (Longworth 1981, figs. 22 & 23) find parallels, in addition to those cited (*Ibid*. 39) from Durrington Walls, Lawford, (Now published by Smith 1985, P87-98), Puddlehill Pit 4 (Matthews 1976, fig. 2, 1 & 2), the Sanctuary and Woodhenge circle 2, in further finds from Willington, Derbys, (Manby 1980, fig. 58) Stonea, Cambridgeshire (Potter 1976, fig. 5.3), Hengistbury Head and Wyke Down, Down Farm, Dorset (Gardiner, 1987, 45-6, ill. 30. P5). New variants are represented by fine bowls with plain exterior but carrying a band of fine twisted cord impressions internally beneath the rim (*N37-40*) and smaller somewhat coarser bowls with two twisted cord lines externally below the rim and a single twisted cord line on top of the rim, (*N14-15, N17-18*).

It is difficult to resist the conclusion that the emphasis upon bowls simply reflects the nature of the site and the use to which the pottery was put, the bowls representing here the personal, easily transportable component of the ceramic assemblage. Selection clearly extended to fine and somewhat less fine wares. Though the context of the decorated bowls from the base of the 1971 shaft may suggest a ritual usage (*vide* Mercer 1981, 23) it is worth noting that the sherds of cord decorated bowls from the chipping floor are of still finer ware while the contexts of comparable incised bowls from Puddle Hill, Willington and Stonea give no obvious grounds for assuming any other function than the purely domestic. While some forms of fine ware may therefore have been selected for ritualistic display, the suggestion that all the bowls with all-over internal decoration were produced for that purpose seems unfounded.

TABLE 1 Occurrence of Grooved Ware recovered during the BM Excavations.

	Context	*No. of sherds*
Area A		
1252.5/905.5	Chipping floor	6
1255.5/905.5	-	41
	3	20+
	Chipping floor	7
	6	1
1260.5/906.1	2	4
	Chipping floor	Bowl *N46*
1260.5/911.1	3	1
1267.5/906.1	F1	35+
β 7	4	1
β 11	3	3
β 13	4	1
	8	5
β 16	6 Chipping floor	18
β 17	6 Chipping floor	1
β 18	4	3
	8	7
β 19	4	1
β 40	6 Chipping floor	1 + Bowl *N46*
Area C		
1313.5/927.5	Topsoil	1
	II	1
1325.5/970.5	2	1
Shaft X		
1270.5/900.5	2	1
	3	1
1270.5/905.5	4	2
1275.5/900.5	9	8
1275.5/905.5	4	1

Illustrated Catalogue

Middle Neolithic Bowl

N1   Rim
74: L462 1325/970 2

Peterborough Ware

N2   Shoulder of soft porous paste, brown externally, brown to grey internally. Decoration: traces of twisted cord herringbone across the shoulder. Armstrong Coll. Pit 12, Floor C.

N3   Rim sherd of well fired paste tempered with crushed flint, brown both faces. Decoration: on the outer rim bevel, rows of bone impressions with further bone impressions set in perhaps a double chevron pattern on the internal surface. Armstrong Coll. Pit 12, Floor C.

N4   Rim sherd of well fired paste tempered with crushed flint, brown to grey externally, brown internally. Decoration: on top of the rim, incised herringbone. On the internal surface, a single bone impression survives. Armstrong Coll. Pit 12, Floor C.

N5   Three wall sherds of soft porous paste one retaining evidence of shell gritting. Decoration: two of the sherds carry blurred herringbone in twisted cord, the other less regular impressions in whipped cord. Armstrong Coll. Pit 12, Floor C.

N6   Wall sherd of well fired paste tempered with crushed flint, greyish brown both faces. Decoration: converging lines of bone impressions. Armstrong Coll. Pit 12, Floor C.

N7   Two rim sherds of soft porous paste, brown externally, brown to grey internally. Decoration: on outer rim bevel, twisted cord herringbone. On the internal edge of the rim and on the surface below, whipped cord herringbone. Armstrong Coll. Pit 12, Floor C. Armstrong (1934) Pl. XII, fig. 4; Armstrong (1932) Pl. IV fig. 3.

N8   Five wall sherds including shoulder of well fired paste tempered with crushed flint grit, brown externally, dark grey to brown internally. Decoration: over the shoulder and body twisted cord herringbone. Armstrong Coll. Pit 12, Floor C.

N9   Wall sherd of well fired paste tempered with crushed flint, brown both faces with dark grey core. Decoration: on the external surface, whipped cord diagonal lines. Armstrong Coll. Pit 12, Floor C. (Not illustrated).

N10   Rim, brown externally, internal surface lost, tempered with some grit. Decoration: on the rim, rows of circumferential impressions. On the neck, a row of vertical impressions. Weathered. (Not illustrated) 73: L116 1263/900.5 H.

N11   Wall sherd. Very weathered. All surfaces lost. Tempered with flint. (Not illustrated) .
73: L118 1263/900.5
Chipping Floor Ea.

Beaker

N12   Rim sherd, tempered with some fine grit, brown both faces. Decoration: on the internal rim bevel, a row of transverse finger nail impressions. Externally, vertical rows of finger pinched rustication. Surface of field S. Side of Grimes Graves. (The Santon Field) 1916 ALA. Peake (1917) 434, fig. 89c. Gibson (1982) 420, fig. 1.
Norwich 63.948

N13   Wall sherd, tempered with some grog, brown both faces with grey core. Decoration: heavy

finger-pinched rustication. Floor 16. Peake (1917) 434, fig. 89d. Gibson (1982) 420, fig. 4.
Norwich 63.948

Grooved Ware

N14   Twenty sherds plus fragments, including five rims, of soft flakey paste, reddish brown. Decoration: externally, remains of one to two twisted cord lines below the rim and a single ?twisted cord line on top of the rim. Layer 5 between chalk blocks, 14-15½′ below the cut edge, in Pit 2.
1917 11-5, 1, 2 & 9

N15   Six sherds including two joining rims, of fairly soft paste, brown externally, brown to grey internally. Decoration: externally, two lines of twisted cord beneath the rim with a single line of twisted cord on top of the rim. Inside gallery 10, 4′ from entrance, close to the right wall and near the floor (Smith (1915) 210, fig. 80), Pit 2.
1917 11-5

N16   Rim sherd of fairly well fired paste tempered with a little grit, greyish brown both faces. Decoration: internal surface shows lightly incised pattern of diagonal lines overlain by crossed lines with horizontal line beneath. Between chalk blocks, layer 5, 17½′ below surface, 6′ from margin of the pit, in Pit 2.
1917 11-5 21

N17   Four sherds plus fragments, including two rims, of soft flakey paste, reddish brown to grey both faces. Decoration: externally, remains of one or more twisted cord lines beneath the rim and a further line of ?twisted cord (smoothed over) on top of the rim. Inside gallery 7, 4′ from entrance, close to right wall and near the floor, in Pit 2.
1917 11-5 11

N18   Eighteen sherds including two rims of soft flakey paste, reddish brown to grey. Decoration: externally, remains of two lines of twisted cord beneath the rim with a single line of twisted cord on top of the rim. Layer 5, 20-23′ from surface, Pit 2.
1917-11-5 13

N19   Two undecorated rims plus fragments of fairly well fired paste, reddish brown. Layer 5, 20-23′ below standard level, in Pit 2.
1917 11-5 12

N20   Nineteen undecorated sherds plus frag-ments including rim of fairly well fired paste, reddish brown. NW side, on level with top of gallery 5, Pit 2.
1917 11-5 3

N21   Three undecorated sherds including rim of well fired paste tempered with some grit, brown externally greyish brown internally. Between chalk blocks in gallery 1, Pit 1.
1917 11-5 15

N22   Twenty undecorated sherds plus fragments, including two rims of well fired paste tempered with some grit, grey to brown both faces, surface smoothed. 27′ deep in layer 8 between chalk blocks, 6′ from E. edge and 2′ from mouth of gallery (one) first opened, in Pit 1.
1917 11-5 16

N23   Eight undecorated sherds plus fragments including sherds of base angle, of soft flakey paste, reddish brown to grey. From above ledge of floor flint under buttress beween galleries 6 and 7, Pit 2.
1917 11-5 10

N24   Twenty-three undecorated sherds plus frag-ments, including five joining rims and three joining base angles, of well fired paste tempered with grit, grey to brown both faces, surface roughly smoothed. 27′ deep (from the) standard level, 2′ from the W. edge, just under the arch S. of (gallery) one first opened, in Pit 1.
1917 11-5 17

N25   Seven undecorated sherds including two rims, of fairly well fired paste tempered with some grog, reddish brown to grey both faces. Gallery 7, Pit 2.
1917 11-5 7

N26   Fifteen undecorated sherds plus fragments, including three joining rim sherds, of fairly well fired paste, brown to grey both faces. Between chalk blocks, 27′ below the top of the mound, in Pit 1.
1917 11-5 19

N27   Twenty undecorated sherds including rim and base of fairly well fired paste tempered with some large flint grits and a little grog, reddish brown both faces with grey core. Both faces heavily scraped. NW side on level with head of gallery 5 and layer 5 between chalk blocks 18′ below standard level, in Pit 2.
1917 11-5, 3, 4 & 4a

N28   Six undecorated sherds plus fragments, including base angle of well fired paste tempered with grit, brown externally, grey to brown internally. Between chalk blocks in gallery 1, Pit 1. (Not illustrated).
1917 11-5 18

N29   Six undecorated wall sherds plus fragments. 2′ above floor of shaft, entrance to gallery 5, Pit 2. (Not illustrated).
1917 11-5 5

N30   Two undecorated wall sherds. Inside gallery 7, Pit 2. (Not illustrated).
1917 11-5 6

N31   Two undecorated wall sherds of fairly soft paste, reddish brown externally, grey internally. 19′ below cut edge in sand at western edge over the entrance to gallery 7, Pit 2. (Not illustrated).
1917 11-5 8

N32   Undecorated wall sherd. 2′ above shaft floor at entrance to gallery 5, Pit 2. (Not illustrated).
1917 11-5 23

N33   Two undecorated wall sherds of fairly soft paste brown both faces tempered with shell. In rubble on west side of gallery 6, 3′ from shaft entrance, in Pit 2. (Not illustrated)
1917 11-5 20

N34   Undecorated fragments. Gallery 7, Pit 2. (Not illustrated)
1917 11-5 14

N35   31 sherds plus fragments including rim and base, from one or more plain bowls, tempered with a little grit. Light brown to grey externally, dark grey to brown internally. NW sector of the shaft, Greenwell Pit.
502 & 658

N36   62 sherds plus fragments including rim and base, from one or more plain bowls of sandy paste tempered with grit including some flint. Light to dark grey to brown patchy. SW gallery, Greenwell Pit. 607, 611, 616, 623, 633, 640 & 654 (sherds from 623 & 633 and from 633 & 654 join).

N37   Rim, brown both faces, tempered with grit. Decoration: internally, six fine twisted cord horizontal lines beneath the rim.
73: L115
1255.5/905.5 D

N38   Rim, brown both faces, tempered with grit. Decoration: internally, six fine twisted cord horizontal lines beneath the rim.
73: L126 & L132
1255.5/905.5 D & Chipping Floor Dc I

N39   Three sherds including rim, brown both faces. Decoration: internally, remains of six fine twisted cord horizontal lines beneath the rim.
74: L482
β16   6 Chipping Floor

N40   Rim, brown both faces, tempered with grit. Decoration: internally, remains of four fine twisted cord horizontal lines beneath the rim.
74: L594
β17   6 Chipping Floor bI

N41   Four sherds including rim, brown both faces. Decoration: internally, remains of three fine twisted cord horizontal lines beneath the rim.
74: L490
β16   6 Chipping Floor dI

N42   Two wall sherds, brown both faces. Decoration: above and below ?shoulder, horizontal incised lines.
74: L338
β11   3

N43   Fourteen undecorated sherds plus fragments, including rim, brown both faces.
73: L134
1255.5/905.5 B

N44   Three undecorated rim sherds, brown externally, grey internally, tempered with a little shell.
72: M274 1260.5/906.1 M
Chalk spread 2

N45   Undecorated rim, brown both faces.
73: L89
1255.5/905.5 A
Chalk rubble 3

N46   Undecorated bowl, brown externally, patchy brown to grey internally, tempered with some grit.
72: M289, M321-30, M334 & 339
73: L104 & L133
74: L395-6

1260.5/906.1 on top & in Chipping Floor Bd II, I, M
& MaII.
β40   6   Chipping Floor

N47   Undecorated rim, brown both faces.
74: L344
β18   4

N48   Undecorated rim, grey externally.
72: LA 197
1260.5/911.1 M
Chalk spread 3

N49   Six undecorated sherds including rim,
brown both faces tempered with some shell.
73: L20
1267.5/906.1 Feature 1

N50   Undecorated base, brown externally, brown
to grey internally, tempered with a little grit including
shell.
73: L20-22
1267.5/906.1 Feature 1

N51   Undecorated base angle, brown both faces.
73: L63
1255.5/905.5

N52   Undecorated base, brown externally, brown
to grey internally, tempered with a little grit.
73: L117 & L135
1255.5/905.5 A
1255.5/900.5 H   6

N53   Undecorated base, brown externally, grey
intenally, tempered with grit.
73: L114
1255.5/905.5 L (hearth)

N54   Undecorated base, brown externally, grey
internally, tempered with a little grit.
73: L42, L83 & L87
1255.5/905.5 K, H   3

N55   Two fragments of undecorated base angle,
brown externally, grey internally, tempered with a
little grit including flint.
73: L63
1255.5/905.5

N56   Rim, brown both faces. Decoration: internally, remains of three fine twisted cord horizontal
lines beneath the rim. (Not illustrated).
74: L584
β40   6   Chipping Floor bI

N57   Rim, brown both faces. Decoration: internally, remains of three fine twisted cord horizontal
lines beneath the rim. (Not illustrated).
74: L576
β16   6   Chipping Floor dII

N58   Undecorated rim, brown externally, grey
internally. (Not illustrated).
73: L127
1252.5/905.5 Chipping Floor DcII

N59   Undecorated base angle, brown externally,
grey internally, tempered with some shell. (Not
illustrated)
74: L530
1270.5/900.5   3

N60   Eight undecorated sherds including base
angle. (Not illustrated)
76: L2385
1275/900   9

N61   Six undecorated sherds including base
angle, brown externally, grey internally. (Not
illustrated).
73: L87
1255.5/905.5   3   K

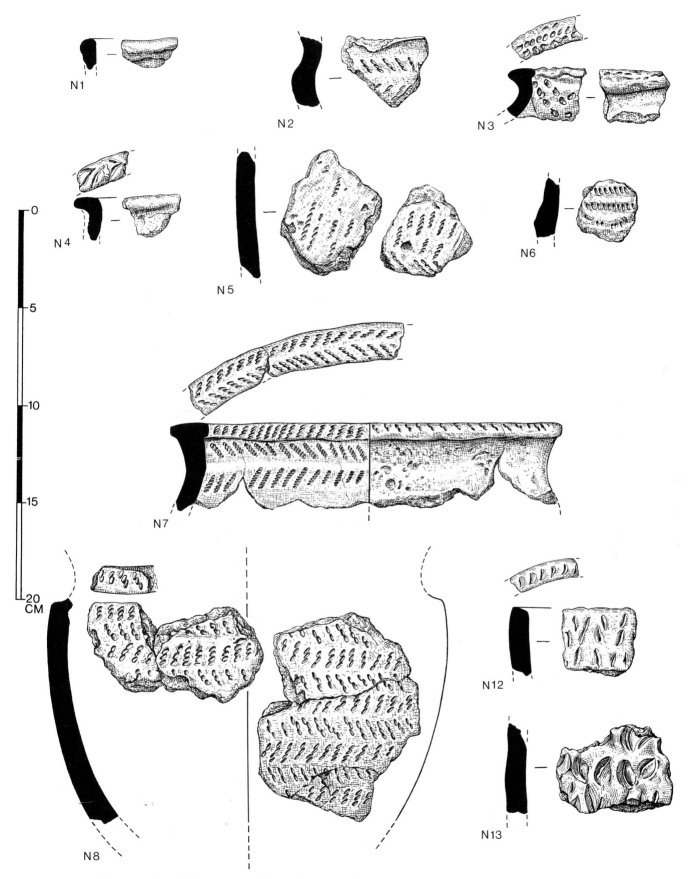

fig. 3   Neolithic pottery: *N1*, plain bowl; *N2-11*, Peterborough Ware; *N12-13*, Beaker.

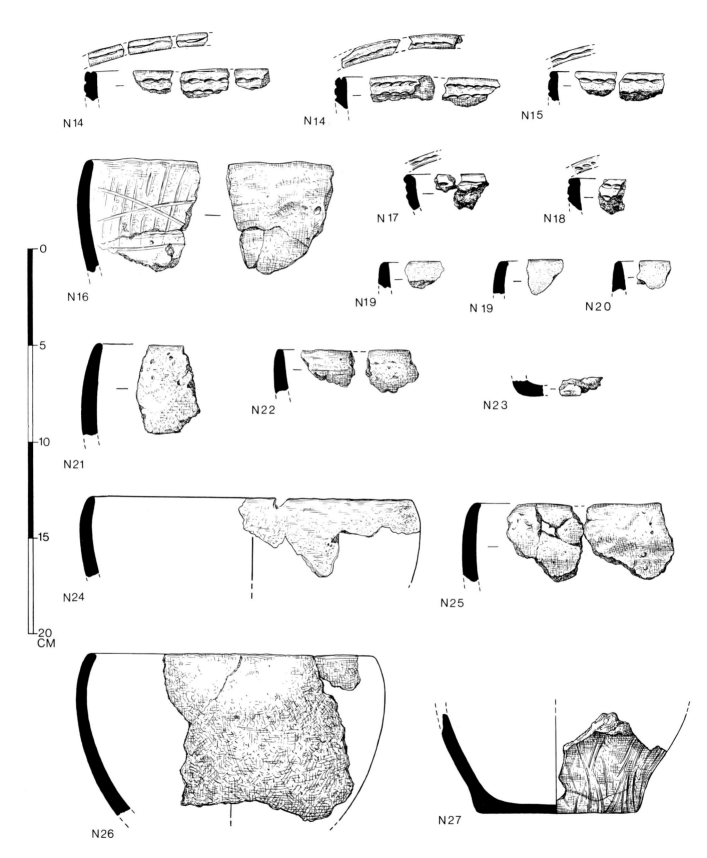

N14   N14   N15

N16   N17   N18

N19   N19   N20

N21   N22   N23

N24   N25

N26   N27

0
5
10
15
20
CM

fig. 4   Neolithic Pottery: *N14-27*, Grooved Ware.

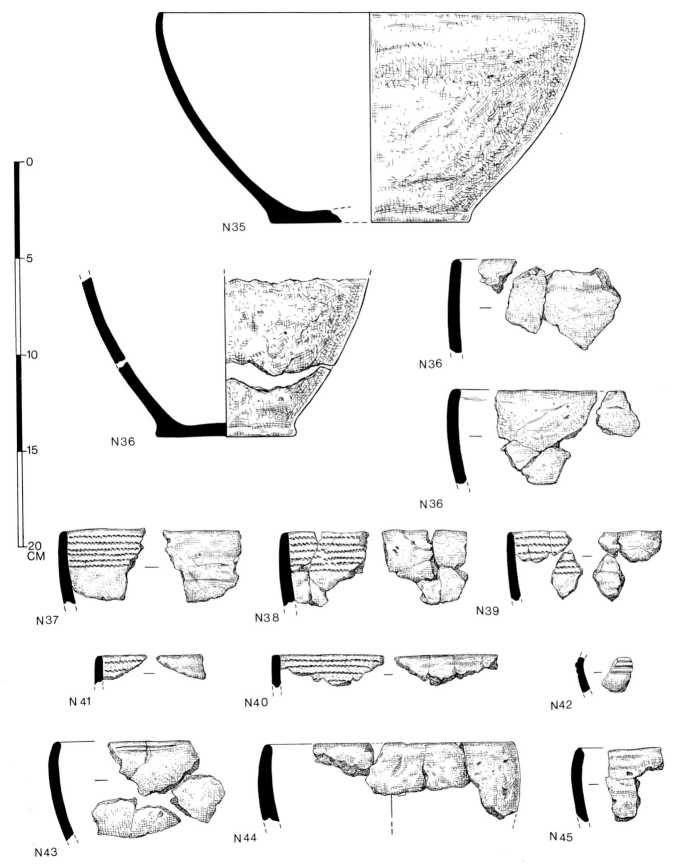

0
5
10
15
20
CM

N35

N36

N36

N36

N37

N38

N39

N41

N40

N42

N43

N44

N45

fig. 5. Neolithic Pottery: *N35–45*, Grooved Ware.

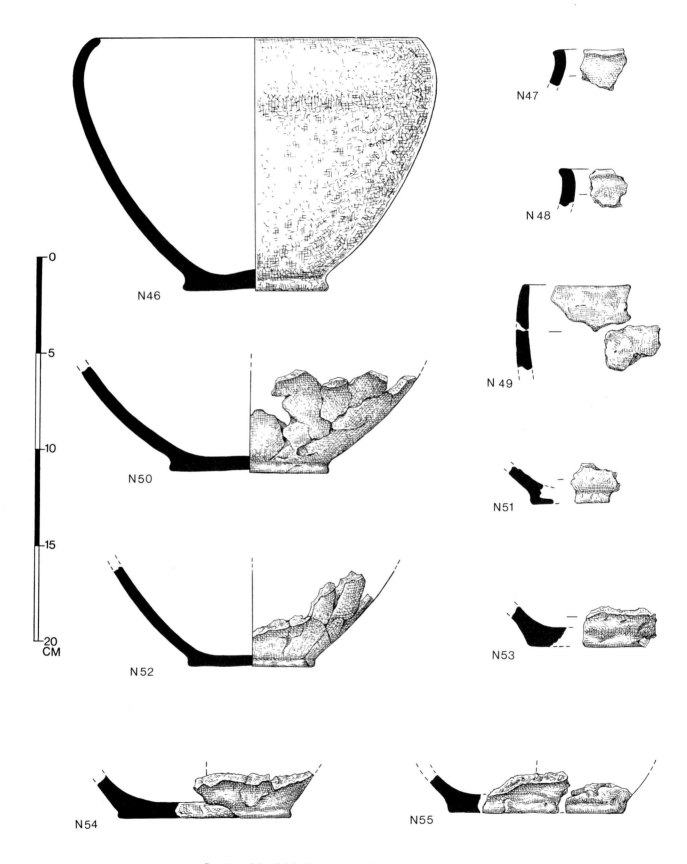

fig. 6   Neolithic Pottery: *N46-55*, Grooved Ware.

II Collared Vessels and other Early Bronze Age Forms

1 Collared Vessels

Some 40 sherds of Collared vessel have been found confined to two localities:-

1) 37 sherds from Sieveking's excavations in the West Field:-

950/950 F33 1 A layer of loamy sand with small amounts of flint and pottery.

950/950 F105 1 A dark sandy layer with small chalk lumps, with scattered flint nodules and flakes forming the top-most filling in the east side of a pit.

950/950 F108 1 A very dark sandy layer with small chalk lumps containing scattered burnt flints, antler, pottery and hammerstones.

940/940 F112 2 A dense area of knapping debris lying in the top of two infilled pits (F112 and F145).

A single sherd was also found in topsoil in cutting 940/950.

2) Three possible sherds from Mercer's excavations in the topmost fills of the 1971 shaft (Longworth 1981: 39).

There is no indication to suppose that this pottery served anything other than a domestic function (Longworth 1984: 76).

2 Other Forms

Some 63 sherds of Early Bronze Age fabric have come from the site: 58 from features 105 & 108 and 5 from the top of the 1971 shaft. These are likely to belong to ancillary domestic vessels but the sherds are in the main too small for useful comment. The thumb pot B8 is very similar to those occurring in funerary contexts with Collared vessels. (Longworth 1984: 55). The clay ball B7 could have served as a pommel or more likely the top of a bow-drill.

Catalogue

Collared Vessels

B1   Two sherds (joining) from base of collar and neck of plain vessel of fairly soft paste, light brown externally, brown internally. (Longworth 1984 no 974).
198 956/956 & 1199 955/958 F 108   1

B2   Plain base angle of similar paste.
170 955/953 F 108   1

B3   Sherd from base of collar of plain vessel, of similar paste, greyish brown both faces. (Longworth 1984 no 975).
164 955/953 F 108   1

B4   Sherd from base of collar, of similar paste, plain.
1428 955/953 F 108   1

B5   Undecorated rim, of similar paste.
1235 950/950 F 108   1

2 Other Forms

B6   Undecorated rim sherd of soft fabric tempered with grit, grey both faces.
1178 955/953 F 108   1

B7   Clay ball with deeply impressed pit. Undecorated.
1346 955/953 F 108   1

B8   Undecorated thumb pot.
1420 957/958 F 108   1

B9   Fragment of undecorated ? spindle whorl.
1170 956/959 F 108   1

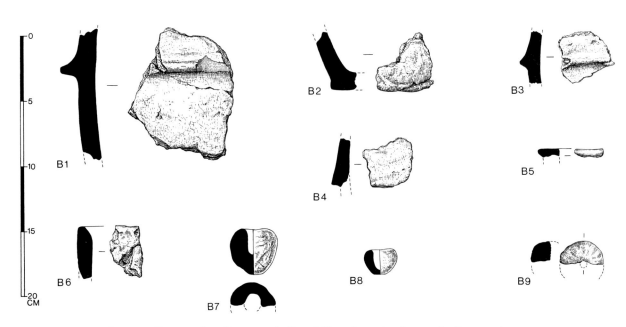

fig. 7   Bronze Age Pottery: Collared Vessels and other early Bronze Age forms: *B1-9.*

III Bucket-Shaped Vessels of the Deverel-Rimbury Tradition

Over 8,000 sherds from Deverel-Rimbury type vessels have been recovered from the site (see Table 2) representing by far the largest domestic assemblage of this type of ware from the British Isles. Of this only the pottery from Mercer's 1971 and 1972 seasons has so far been published (Longworth 1981: 39ff). The vast bulk of this pottery is now housed in the British Museum but the opportunity has been taken to incorporate sherds held also by the Norwich Castle Museum.

1 SUMMARY OF CONTEXTS

Floor 15 (fig. 2) excavated 1915 and 1916. Sherds in Norwich Museum. A Neolithic chipping floor extended over an area of 18 x 16′ lying 1 - 3′ below the surface and resting on sand above boulder clay. Into this Bronze Age hearths had later been inserted associated with pottery, "bones of domestic animals, red and roe deer with teeth of pig, horse and sheep". One sherd of Early Iron Age pottery survives as well as 15 sherds of bucket-shaped vessel comprising 556-8, 4 sherds of base angle and 8 undecorated wall sherds.

Peake (1916) 271-4
Peake (1917) 412 and 434
Peake (1919) 77-82 and 92-3

Floor 16 (fig. 2) excavated 1915-1916 and 1922. Pottery in Norwich Museum and in the British Museum. At a depth of 2½ - 3′ below the surface, over-lain by sand, was a layer containing charcoal, calcined bones, pot boilers, burnt flint and flint chipping, lying on chalk rubble. Remains of a hearth were recovered with bones and teeth of red deer. The site extended over an area some 29 x 24′. A tanged bronze spearhead was found 20″ below the surface on the eastern edge of the site, associated with a later hearth accompanied by charcoal, pot boilers, 'bones of red and roe deer with those of domesticated animals'.

By 1917, about 20 pieces of pottery were said to have come from the site from 'near the hearths which had been inserted through the miners' level'. Single sherds of Rusticated Beaker and Grooved Ware (see p.12) survive but the bulk of the pottery is of bucket-shaped vessels including 559-565, one base angle, one fragment of base and 22 plain wall sherds. Of later wares, 2 sherds of Early Iron Age pottery and 3 sherds of Roman also survive (see p.106).

Peake (1916) 274-87
Peake (1917) 412 ff
Peake (1919) 82-5, 92
Armstrong (1921) 434
Kendall (1925) 64

Floor 42 (A & B) (approximate position see fig. 2) excavated 1919, 1920 and apparently 1927. Eight sherds in Norwich Museum. Little information is preserved about this feature. It lay north of the Tumulus pit and between this and Section 7, probably joining with Floor 85 and is known to have yielded a flint crust engraving. A note with the pottery from 42A reads 'north side of Floor 42. 1919-20. Pottery. Floor of pot boilers. Bones of red deer, two horns red deer, jaws small sheep, ox horn core … polished tine, pin, chalk lamp'.

A and B would indicate more than one chipping floor horizon, A being the uppermost.

The surviving sherds comprise 566, 2 plain sherds from bucket-shaped vessels and 2 joining sherds from an Early Iron Age globular jar, all marked 42A. A fragment of shoulder cordon and 2 plain wall sherds from bucket-shaped vessels are marked 42 or 42B.

Armstrong (1921) 434, fig. A12

Armstrong's ms letter 4/39

Floor 79 (approximate position see fig. 2) excavated 1920. Pottery in Norwich Museum. According to a label preserved with the pottery the site lay to the north of Floor 42 and east of Floor 81. Pottery found 'with pot boilers and charcoal and bones and small flint flakes. 1920 .... above Grimes Graves factory level'. An ms list adds "Bronze Age hearth". Surviving pottery comprises *567* and 3 plain wall sherds of bucket-shaped vessels.

Floor 80 (approximate position see fig. 2) excavated 1930. Pottery in Norwich Museum. Near and to the north of Floor 42. In a surviving letter the site is described as a living site with pot boilers and Bronze Age pottery including 'part of the lip of a thick pot with fingernail on the rim and 2 perforations' (not surviving) also a chalk lamp, a point of a polished bone pin, bones of red deer, sheep, ox and the teeth of a carnivorous animal. An ? associated chipping floor was half buried in sand. Surviving pottery consists of *568*, another plain rim and 9 plain wall sherds of bucket-shaped vessels.

Armstrong's ms letter 1/20.

Floor 85 A, B and C (fig. 2), excavated 1920, 1921 and 1922. Pottery in the British Museum. The site was examined over an area of 109 sq yds down to a depth of at least 3'. Early Iron Age and Roman pottery were said to have been found in the top soil. Three horizons were recognised separated by sterile layers:

A Uppermost up to 6" thick, 1' below the surface lying on sandy chalk rubble. Black humic deposit with charcoal and pot boilers. The layer included hearths, one of which yielded a pair of bronze tweezers (Armstrong (1921), 436, fig. B9) and domestic rubbish including bone tools, Bronze Age pottery and animal bones. The layer was concentrated in the eastern and north-eastern sectors of the site but was absent to the south.

B 1' 9" below the surface lay a chipping floor 7-9" thick, containing several small hearths, animal bones and teeth, mainly of 'red deer and ox' and antler picks. In one restricted area there appeared to be evidence

for antler pick manufacture. The layer was thickest in the southern sector of the site.

C At a depth of 2'6" below the surface lay a second chipping floor 3 - 5" thick which had extended originally over the area of the Tumulus pit (which cut through it) and as far as Floor 42. It contained a hearth 4' in diameter at its western end. Near the centre was 'the base of an earthenware vessel of about 9" diameter, made of coarse pottery much burnt and shattered, and too fragile for removal in its entirety'. Other fragments of pot also recovered included several sherds 'forming portions of the base and side of a vase' (said to be identical to the pottery found in pits 1 and 2 excavated in 1914), in a pocket beneath Floor 85C. This floor, which also yielded flint crust engravings, thinned out towards the south of the area opened.

The surviving pottery consists of a rim sherd of plain Middle Neolithic bowl marked Floor 85 and a probable wall sherd from Floor 85A. 10 sherds of bucket-shaped vessels: *569-571*, together with 4 undecorated wall sherds, survive from Floor A. *572* and an undecorated wall sherd from Floor C as well as two unlocated wall sherds. There are also 2 sherds of Early Iron Age pottery labelled as from Floor C, a sherd of Roman jar from Floor A and sherds of Samian and Dalesware unlocated but presumably from the topsoil.

Armstrong   (1921)   434

Armstrong   (1922)   548-58

Armstrong   (1924c)   194-202

Armstrong   (1927)   99-101

Floor 86 (fig 2) said to have been one of the 'earliest factory sites'. No other data. One sherd *573* in Norwich Museum.

Armstrong (1927) 121, fig. 1.

Kent's Low Floor (not precisely located). Pottery in the British Museum. A note with this states 'it proved later to be an entension of the Black Hole'. 13 sherds of bucket-shaped vessel survive from this feature: *574-5* and 11 undecorated wall sherds, together with fragments of loomweight (L1). The site also yielded a bronze spiral finger-ring. A sherd of Medieval jar also survives.

Section South West of Black Hole (not precisely located). Pottery in the British Museum. 8 sherds of bucket-shaped vessel survive: *576-8* and 3 undecorated wall sherds. 20+ sherds of an Early Iron Age shouldered jar also come from this feature.

Section 7 (fig 2) Excavated 1914. Pottery in the British Museum. A trench 4' x 6' was made on the edge of a concealed shaft and taken to a depth of 9'. The pit, which lay at the Western end of what was later to be called Floor 85, contained an occupation layer up to 3' thick at the centre containing charcoal, pottery, pot boilers, bone pins, bones of sheep and goat, red and roe deer.

147 sherds of bucket-shaped vessel survive comprising *279 - 303* and 113 undecorated wall sherds but the sherd illustrated by Clarke (1915) fig 82 cannot be traced. There is also one sherd of Early Iron Age flint tempered ware in Norwich Museum marked as from this site.

Clarke (1915), 115-8 and 212-3.
Peake (1916) 275
Peake (1917) 410

Pit 3 (fig 2) Excavated 1917. Pottery in Norwich Museum. A section cut across the pit revealed flint waste 'bones of red deer and one tooth of a carnivorous animal, either a fox or dog and jaw of a sheep or goat' in the uppermost 2' above a layer of fine chalk rubble, 1½' thick. Through this second layer ran a band of charcoal 'evidently a hearth with bones of red deer'. 2 types of pottery are said to have come from this hearth.

A base-angle and 4 undecorated wall sherds of bucket-shaped vessel are in Norwich Museum labelled as from 'hearth 3' deep in pit 3.', as well as a rim sherd, *579*, labelled as from 'hearth in pit near midden north of Floor 15.'. This is almost certainly the sherd described as from the hearth in pit 3 (Peake (1919), fig 87B).

Peake (1919) 86-7.

Pit 6 (not precisely located) wall sherd of bucket-shaped pottery in Norwich Museum. The pit is referred to in ms list 'South West part of graves. Lingwood's section'. A sherd from an Early Iron Age fine shouldered jar also survives.

Pit 12 (fig. 2) excavated 1928, 1930 and 1932-3. Pottery in the British Museum. A masked mine shaft, 18' deep with 8 galleries. 7 chipping horizons are recorded in the fill labelled A to G (see section: Armstrong (1934) fig. 3), A being the latest. '2 small fragments of Neolithic pottery, undecorated' are said to come from Floor B which also included 3 hearths and bones of sheep and ox. From Floor C came fragments of a Peterborough Bowl (see above p.12), one fragment being from the sandy lip of the pit beneath Floor B, and sherds of three other bowls (one plain and 2 decorated). A fragment of 'plain pottery was found at 12' amidst chalk rubble (ie between floors E to F, but no pottery occurred beneath that level'.

29 sherds plus fragments of undecorated wall and flat base from bucket shaped vessels survive from Floor C. The presence of one Peterborough sherd from the lip of the pit beneath Floor B may indicate that the Neolithic sherds in Floor C have been redeposited.

Armstrong (1932) 59-61
Armstrong (1934) 382-94

Black Hole (fig. 2) pottery in the British Museum. One sherd in Norwich Museum. Discovered 1922; excavated 1924-1925 and 1926. The site had already been disturbed and was further disturbed by a 'Dutch professor' (Armstrong (1927), 95). The site lay in the weathering cone of a mine shaft 31' in diameter, and was explored to a depth of 11', "of which 9'6" was an accumulation of charcoal-ash and household debris, bones, pottery, flint and bone tools, vessels and objects of chalk, personal ornament and many thousands of pot boilers".

Armstrong dug the feature using a grid system numbering the 3' squares 9 through 0 to 1A and from A to H (fig. 8). Where the material is marked, the depth is added in feet, the figure for the depth normally being the first. When the material was later marked, the depth was sometimes made the last component thus B63, 6B3 and 3B6 can mean the same thing.

A schematic section through the feature was published by Armstrong in his Presidential address (1927, fig. 32). This indicates a layer of chalk mining debris beneath the Bronze Age deposits demonstrating that Armstrong was correct in his first interpretation of the site as lying in the weathering cone of a mine shaft and mistaken in his later view that the site lay in a hollow between sand dunes.

A total of 1,801 sherds of bucket-shaped pottery survives from the feature. It should be noted however, that compared to the excavated assemblages recovered by Mercer and Longworth, the Armstrong collection is heavily weighted towards large sherds suggesting that small sherds were often discarded. 21 fragments of cylindrical loomweight were also recovered.

TABLE 2: Occurrence of bucket-shaped pottery from Grimes Graves

Context	No. of Sherds		Cutting	Layer	No. of sherds
Longworth excavations:-				5 (=F9)	54
Shaft X	3017		1275.5/905.5	Topsoil 1	2
Area A	48			F1	9
Area B	14			F3	1
Area C	56			2	26
Mercer's 1971&1972 excavations	2974			3	6
Armstrong's Black Hole	1801*			Total 212	
Section 7	147				
Floor 15	15				
Floor 16	31		*Phase II*		
Floor 42 or 42B	3				
Floor 42A	3		1270/900	13	244
Floor 79	4			14	71
Floor 80	11			15	16
Floor 85	1			16	69
Floor 85A	7			17	28
Floor 85C	2			18	315
Floor 86	1			19	16
				19a	28
Kent's Low Floor	13			19b	29
Section SW of Black Hole	8			19c	100
				20	145
Pit 3	6			20a	316
Pit 6	1			20/21	11
Pit 12 Floor C	29			21	8
No provenance	10			22	17
			1270.5/905.5	3	54
Sieveking's Excavations:-				4	152
880/910 2	21			4a	7
	Total 8223			9	28
			1275.5/900.5	4	113
*See comment on size of sherds p.27.				6	6
				7	5
			1275.5/905.5	4	211
				5	190
				6	324
				6a	11
				10	12
			β 41	4	10
				5	10
				6	10
			β 42	5	11
				6	29
			β 43	4	2
				5	12
				6	41
			β 44	5	4
				6	36
			β 48	4	2
			β 49	4	2
				Total 2695	

TABLE 3   Occurrence of bucket-shaped Bronze Age pottery recovered during the excavation of Shaft X and Areas A, B &C.

SHAFT X

Phase I

Cutting	Layer	No. of sherds
1270/900	1	8
	2	57
	12	13
1270.5/905.5	Topsoil 1	18
	Topsoil 3	9
	2	2
1275.5/900.5	Topsoil 1	1
	2	4
	3	2

TABLE 3   Cont.

Phase III

1270/900	23a	2
	26	1
1275.5/900.5	9	1
	14	4
	15	5
1275.5/905.5	12	3
		—
	Total	16
		—

Not Phased

1270/900	3	17
	Unstrat.	47
1270.5/905.5	2/3/4	5
	6	1
	10	3
	Unstrat.	3
1275.5/900.5	11	5
1275.5/905.5	3/4	3
	7	7
	11	4
		—
	Total	95
		—

AREA A

1255.5/911.1	5	1
	Unstrat.	2
1260.5/911.1	5	1
1266/900.5	2	1

	Unstrat.	1
β 7	2	3
β 11	2	2
	3	1
β 12	2	3
	3	1
β 13	3	2
	4	1
	8	4
β 14	4	2
β 18	3	1
	4	2
	8	4
	Unstrat.	10
β 19	Unstrat.	5
β 40	2	1

AREA B

1285/910	Topsoil	13
	8	1

AREA C

1313.5/927.5	Topsoil	1
	Topsoil 2	1
1325.5/967.5	2	2
	3	2
1325.5/970.5	2	10
	3	1
	4	5
	6	3
	7	28
1325.5/973.5	2/3	1
1327.5/1040.5	2	1
1330.5/970.5	2	1

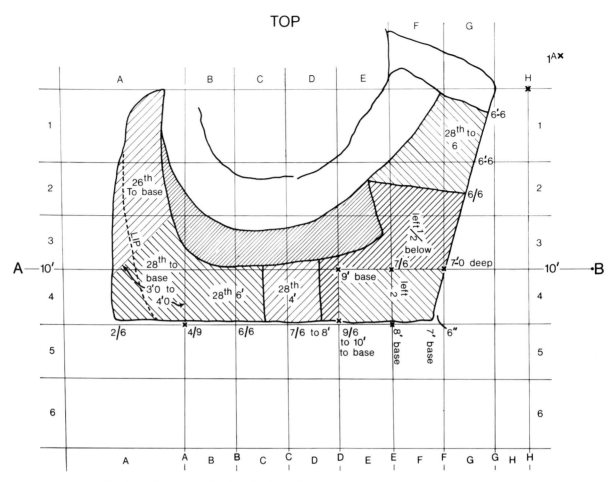

fig. 8   Armstrong's sketch plan of the Black Hole under excavation with grid reference used.

TABLE 4: Samples of charcoal submitted for C14 dating from Shaft X

BM Number	Area	Level & Square	Uncalibrated bc	Calibrated (following Pearson and Stuiver)
BM 1035	1270/900	14G	1044 + 40	1310-1210, 1175-1165
1036	1270/900	19G	1045 + 39	1310-1210, 1175-1165
1037	1270.5/905.5	9JMN	1053 + 49	1375-1340, 1320-1210, 1175-1165
1038	1275.5/905.5	5A	986 + 43	1255-1055
1039	1270/900	20M	856 + 54	1025-905
1040	1270/900	20aD	955 + 54	1250-1245, 1215-1005
1041	1270/900	19aC	1623 + 57	2025-1880
1042	1270/900	19bH	969 + 53	1255-1235, 1220-1025
1043	1270/900	19cH	888 + 53	1060-920
1263	1270.5/905.5	4L	1493 + 53	1875-1685
★1264	1270.5/905.5	10	1204 + 64	1510-1395
1265	1275.5/900.5	4 B-D, F-H	850 + 79	1045-845
1266	1275.5/905.5	6K	884 + 53	1050-920

★All dates are for Phase II with the exception of BM 1264 which comes from an unassigned layer.

Over 60 sherds of Early Iron Age pottery from five vessels also survive as well as a sherd of Late Bronze Age fabric and sherds from nine Roman vessels. The Roman sherds are all unmarked and were presumably derived from the humic top-soil layer. Several of the Iron Age sherds are, however, marked and this would indicate derivation from the upper part of the lowest of the three layers indicated on the section. The sherds are confined to squares E3 - 5, F4, 5 and 7 and D3 - 5. Without details of the actual excavation it is not now possible to make any conclusive interpretation. At face value these sherds might suggest that the basal layer (if a single layer) was still open in the Iron Age but since the pottery occurs in a restricted area and comprises sherds from only six vessels, it seems more likely that a later pit has gone unnoticed by the excavators which intruded into the top of the lowest layer.

Armstrong   (1924) 192-3
Armstrong   (1927) 107-109

British Museum Excavations 1972-6

(a)   Shaft X (figs. 2, 9-11) (Cuttings 1270/900, 1270.5/905.5, 1275.5/900.5 & 1275.5/905.5)
Over 3000 sherds of bucket-shaped pottery were recovered during excavations begun in 1972 with further seasons in 1974-6 of shaft X, a concealed mine-shaft on the southern margin of the site. Their occurrence by phase and layer is given in Table 3.

The uppermost levels of the weathering cone of the shaft consisted of humic fills with varying degrees of sand admixture, reaching at the centre a depth of 1.6m. It is probable that at some stage the natural accumulation of soil within the cone was enhanced by deliberate in-filling to level-off the top, but the date of this infilling could not be established. Towards the base of these superficial humic deposits, prehistoric pottery, flint-working debris and animal bone became more concentrated. It was evident, however, that these deposits had been mixed and re-worked, and the finds from these have been treated as unstratified.

Between the superficial layers and the beginnings of the chalk rubble infill of the mine-shaft proper a series of layers could be defined representing discrete acts of tipping interspersed between periods of rapid accumulation. Three deposits of midden material, rich in Bronze Age pottery, struck flint, animal bone, calcined flint and charcoal could be isolated, Midden I tipped from the NE, Midden II from the W and Midden III from the SW respectively. The speed at which these deposits were being formed is shown clearly by the interdigitation of the tip lines (e.g. layer 9a in 1270.5/905.5) within the general accumulation represented by layer 4 (fig. 10). Much of the cutting 1275.5/900.5 was composed of an accumulation of wind-blown sand incorporating a considerable quantity of faunal refuse lying against the south eastern side of the cone, and it is clear that movement of sand could have led to rapid in-filling. A series of samples of charcoal taken for C14 dating from different layers in these deposits gave ages clustering between 1053 and 850bc (Burleigh *et al*, 1979, 45, V b [ii]). On calibration, however, these dates expand to fall, with the exception of two, within the bracket 1375-845BC (see Table 4). The incorporation into these deposits of a small number of sherds which, on temper and technique, might be placed some five centuries later than the bucket-shaped pottery is discussed on p.104.

Exploration was taken down into the Neolithic mine-shaft only as far as was necessary to establish that the Bronze Age episode had been fully explored. Material recovered can thus be assigned to one of three broad phases: phase II, the period during which deliberate Bronze Age infilling was taking place; phase III a preceding phase represented by the pre-Bronze Age layers of the Neolithic mine-shaft, and phase I the subsequent post-Bronze Age accumulations.

Previous disturbance (fig. 11)
Exploration of cutting 1270.5/905.5 revealed that the site had previously been examined by way of a sub-rectangular pit measuring 2.4m by 2.25m which penetrated through the deposit to a maximum depth of 1.85m. It is not possible to establish with certainty when this cutting was made or by whom, but it could have been one of the trial holes dug by E T Lingwood at unrecorded locations on the south side of the Graves in 1923 (Armstrong (1924a) 125) or one of the line of sections cut by Armstrong himself between Floor 88 and the Black Hole.

(b)   Area A (figs. 2, 9 & 11) (Cuttings 1252.5/905.5, 1255.5/900.5;   1255.5/905.5;   1255.5/911.1; 1258/900.5; 1260.5/906.1; 1260.5/911.1; 1263/900.5; 1263/905.5; 1265.5/912.5; 1266/900.5; 1267.5/906.1 & β1-40).

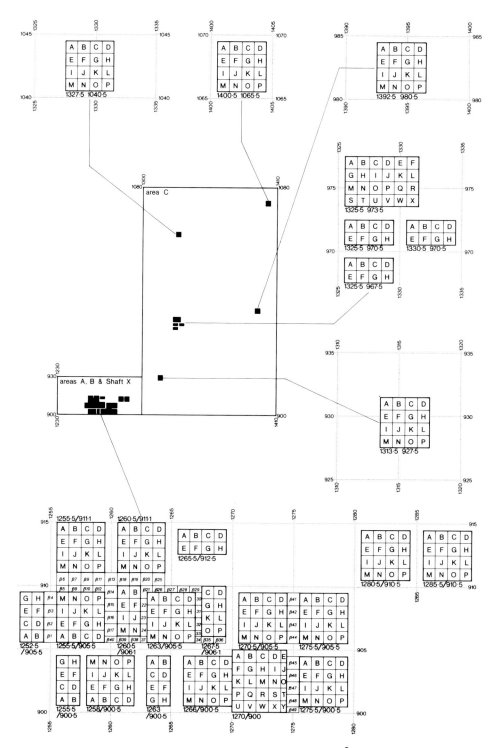

fig. 9   Location map of Areas A, B and C with m^2 reference grid.

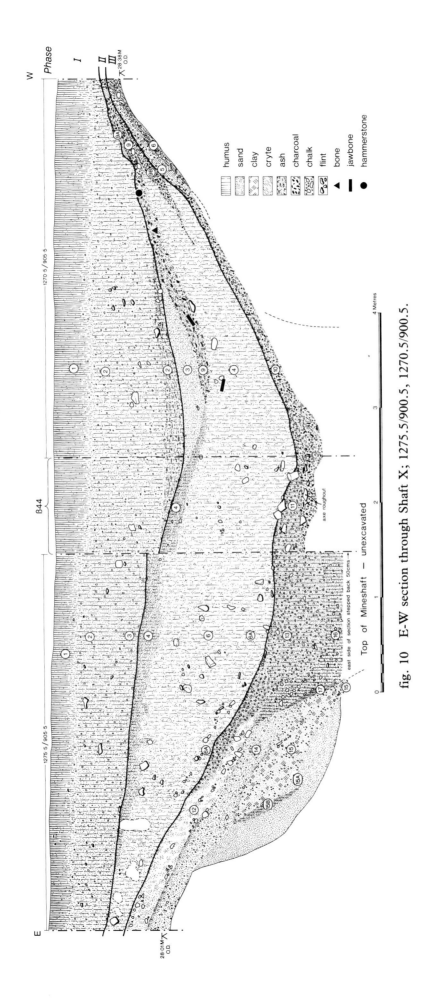

fig. 10 E-W section through Shaft X; 1275.5/900.5, 1270.5/900.5.

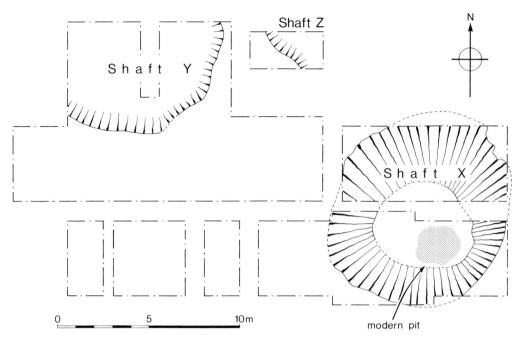

fig. 11 Plan of area A and Shaft X showing relative positions of Shafts X, Y and Z.

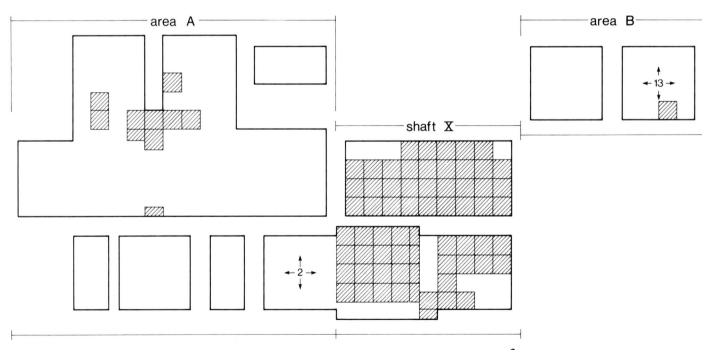

fig. 12 Distribution of Bronze Age Bucket-shaped vessels by m^2 in Areas A, B and Shaft X.

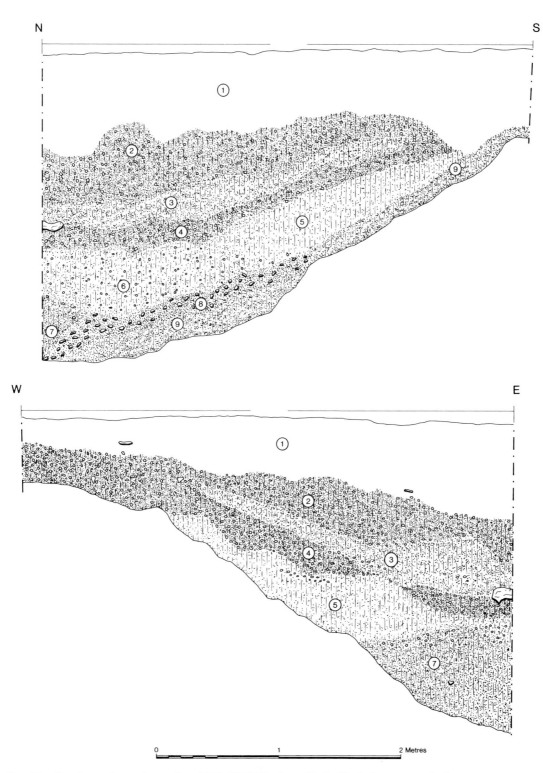

fig. 13 Sections through cutting 1313.5/927.5, Area C: **1**. Dark brown sandy loam.
2. Brown sandy loam with diminuted chalk. **3**. Grey/brown sandy loam. **4**. Similar to 2
above. **5**. Light grey/brown sandy loam. **6**. Similar to 5 above with chalk flecks; merges
with 7. **7**. Mid brown sandy loam. **8**. Flint in light brown sand. **9**. Orange/brown loamy sand.

One of the features revealed by a magnetometer survey carried out in 1972 proved on examination to be the weathering cone of a second concealed mine-shaft (Y). A third concealed mine (Z) also lay nearby (fig. 11). Further cuttings were added in 1973 to explore the extensive Neolithic flint working area to the south associated with sherds of Grooved Ware.

A scatter of sherds of bucket-shaped vessels was recovered from cuttings 1255.5/911.1, 1260.5/911.1 and from baulks β7, β11-14, β18-19 & β40 mainly from superficial levels. These may relate to Bronze Age occupation debris deposited in the top of Shaft Y, though no deposits *in situ* were recovered. The clear separation of this scatter from the deposits in Shaft X and the two sherds recovered from the adjoining cutting (1266/900.5) (fig. 12) suggests that no Bronze Age occupation occurred to any appreciable extent between Shafts X & Y since some residual trace might have been expected to survive in the superficial layers even if the original horizon had largely been destroyed, viz by ploughing, evidence for which was recovered.

(c) Area B (fig. 9) (Cuttings 1280/910 & 1285/910)

In 1976 two further $4m^2$ cuttings were opened to the north-east of Shaft X to test whether any remnant Bronze Age occupation could be traced in that direction. No such occupation was established but 14 sherds of bucket-shaped pottery were recorded, 13 from the the top-soil and a single sherd from layer 8 in cutting 1285/910, an unsealed layer lying immediately on natural.

(d) Area C (fig. 9) (Cuttings 1313.5/927.5; 1325.5/967.5; 1325.5/970.5; 1325.5/973.5; 1327.5/1040.5; 1330.5/970.5; 1392.5/980.5 & 1400.5/1065.5)

A series of small exploratory cuttings (1313.5/927.5; 1327.5/1040.5; 1392.5/980.5 & 1400.5./1065.5) was placed in the area to the east of the main visible mine field to test whether traces of occupation or workshop sites were likely to survive in this area. In addition, a group of cuttings was placed in the vicinity of Armstrong's Floor 85 which was said by the excavator to have shown a clear stratigraphy (cuttings 1325.5/967.5; 1325.5/970.5; 1325.5/973.5 & 1330.5/970.5).

1313.5/927.5

A $4m^2$ cutting revealed a hollow filled with layers of sand and sandy loam in an area of deep sand cover (fig. 13). This hollow was explored down to a depth of 2.4m. No trace of chalk rubble or other mining debris was recorded. The hollow may have been a natural feature amidst dunes but this was not conclusively demonstrated. Two sherds of bucket-shaped vessels were recovered from superficial levels.

Cuttings 1327.5/1040.5; 1392.5/1040.5 & 1400.5/1065.5

These $4m^2$ cuttings, placed at random, all revealed disturbed soil overlying natural to a maximum depth of 55 cms. A single sherd of bucket-shaped vessel came from 1327.5/1040.5. No further work was attempted in this area.

Cuttings 1325.5/967.5; 1325.5/970.5; 1325.5/973.5 & 1330.5/970.5

These cuttings revealed the edge of a concealed mine-shaft (fig. 14). Twenty-six sherds of bucket-shaped pottery came from superficial and disturbed levels and a further 28 from layer 7 in cutting 1325.5/970.5 - a deposit of domestic refuse including charcoal, bone and flint thrown down the side of the weathering cone of the mine-shaft from the south and south-east.

2 DISCUSSION - *ANN ELLISON*

(a) Typology

Owing to the occurrence of many large sherds, especially in the Armstrong Collection from the Black Hole, it has been possible to reconstruct in part a far larger number of vessels than was achieved for Mercer's 1971/72 assemblage (Longworth 1981: 39ff). However, many vessels were still represented only by a single identifiable sherd and even the more complete by very few fragments.

The main characteristic traits represented in the two major assemblages (from the Black Hole and Shaft X respectively) are summarised in Tables 5 and 6 where they are expressed as a percentage of featured sherds (excluding base angles) correct to the nearest whole number. Table 7 compares these percentages with those obtained for the 1971/72 assemblage (Longworth 1981: Table VII) and demonstrates most forcefully the remarkable homogeneity of the three assemblages. The combinations of the various traits found in the Black Hole and Shaft X assemblages are shown in Tables 8 and 9.

Plain rims are common but, wherever evidence for lower areas of the vessel survive, they are associated with cordons, other shoulder decoration, rows of perforations or applied knobs. When decorated, the rims are most often ornamented with finger-tip impressions or incised diagonal lines, the two forms of motif occurring in approximately equal proportions. However, there are slightly more examples of rims bearing diagonal lines in the Black Hole assemblage and more finger-impressed rims in the Shaft X group (see Table 7). Incised diagonal lines are sometimes located on the outer edge of the rim and more complex decorative schemes such as opposed incisions (147) occur rarely.

Rim forms fall into three main classes: bevelled, flattened and rounded. Vessels bearing an internal rim bevel are not common but occur to a significant degree both in the Black Hole (42, 138, 152, 173, 179, 190, 234, 236) and Shaft X (338, 405, 438, 559) assemblages. These rims usually carry incised line or finger-tip decoration upon the bevel. The other two rim types, flattened and rounded, may be plain or decorated and are subdivided as follows:-

Rim type	Black Hole examples Cat. No.	Shaft X examples Cat. No.
Flattened		
straight	4	372
internally expanded	76	364
externally expanded	133	365
T-shaped	148,163	367,368
incurved	7	290
Rounded		
straight	21	309
T-shaped	145	409
incurved	129	326
everted	45,199	332
shallow-necked	60,61,63	-

All these variations occur commonly in both assemblages, except the rounded shallow-necked form which occurs only in the Black Hole group. The

rim types belong to usually straight-sided bucket-shaped vessels of simple form and coarse construction. However, amongst the Black Hole collection there also occurs a small series of pots with a biconical profile, some with a sharp shoulder (e.g. 236, 241, 243) and others displaying a weaker bipartite form (e.g. 36, 73, 155, 199, 242, 287).

On all vessel forms the characteristic decoration comprises a shoulder cordon, usually decorated with finger-tip decoration or, less often, incised diagonal or herringbone lines. The other main types of decoration represented are a row of perforations through the wall between the rim and shoulder and applied knobs. In one case (465) such a knob was perforated horizontally to form a simple lug. Rows of perforations were less common in these two assemblages than in the 1971/72 collection (Table 7) but the occurrence of knobbed vessels was fairly uniform. Both these forms of decoration were associated with plain and decorated rims, excepting the 16 knobbed vessels in the Shaft X assemblage which were characterised by plain rims only (see Tables 8 and 9). In the Shaft X assemblage only, some shoulders were embellished with a directly applied row of finger-tip impressions, a trait which was also noted in the 1971/72 group, and plain shoulder cordons were also represented (516-519). The slight curvature displayed on some of these sherds (516 and 519) suggests that these may represent fragments of arc handles. Other forms of decorative technique represented more occasionally amongst the assemblages include round-toothed comb-point impressions (247) and finger-nail impressions (234, 237, 238) in the Black Hole collection and heavy or light scoring found in both groups (258, 259, 472, 512, 513, 528). In addition, four sherds displayed drill holes, bored after firing, and thus designed most probably to facilitate vessel repair.

(b) Fabric
The fabrics of all feature sherds have been analysed according to a system used by the author to characterise later Bronze Age pottery in Southern England (Ellison 1975). This system employs a simple grading of filler types which is designed to test the techniques of clay preparation developed by individual potters or communities rather than the place of origin of the inclusions identified. The grading system abbreviations used in the catalogue are explained below and it should be noted that the coding (e.g. 3 S Sh) is always presented in the order: density, fragment size, filler type.

TABLE 5 Black Hole: Main characteristic traits expressed as a percentage of featured sherds

Trait

1	Plain rim	37%
2	Finger-tipped shoulder cordon	20%
5	Incised diagonal lines on top of rim	16%
15	Incised diagonal lines on shoulder cordon	6%
3	Perforations between rim and shoulder	6%
7	Applied knobs	6%
14	Comb impressions	4%
12	Finger-nail impressions	4%
4	Finger-tipping on top of rim	4%
9	Incised herringbone on shoulder cordon	3%
8	Other impressions on top of rim	3%
16	Light scoring	2%
10	Incised diagonal lines on outer edge of rim	1%
	All other features (individually) less than	1%

TABLE 6 Shaft X: Main characteristic traits expressed as a percentage of featured sherds

Trait

1	Plain rims	41%
2	Finger-tipped shoulder cordon	14%
4	Finger-tipping on top of rim	14%
5	Incised diagonal lines on top of rim	9%
3	Perforations between rim and shoulder	8%
15	Incised diagonal lines on shoulder cordon	6%
7	Applied knobs	4%
13	Finger-tipping on shoulder	3%
10	Incised diagonal lines on outer edge of rim	2%
16	Heavy scoring	2%
17	Plain shoulder	1%
	All other features (individually) less than	1%

TABLE 7 Percentage occurrence of traits in the Shaft X, Black Hole and 1971/2 assemblages

	Trait	% *Shaft X*	% *Black Hole*	% *Mercer's 1971/2 Assemblage*
1	Plain rims	41	37	39
2	Finger-tipped shoulder cordon	14	20	14
3	Perforations between rim and shoulder	8	6	12
4	Finger tipping on top of the rim	14	4	9
5	Incised diagonal lines on top of rim	9	16	8
6	Impressions other than finger-tipping on shoulder cordon	‹1	‹1	6
7	Applied knobs	4	6	5
8	Other impressions on top of rim	‹1	3	5
9	Incised herringbone on shoulder cordon	‹1	3	4
10	Incised diagonal lines on outer edge of rim	2	1	3
11	Drill holes	‹1	‹1	3
12	Finger-nail impressions	–	4	‹1
13	Finger-tipping on shoulder	3	–	2
14	Comb impressions	–	4	2
15	Incised diagonal lines on shoulder cordon	6	6	‹1
16	{ Heavy scoring	2	‹1	‹1
	{ Light scoring	‹1	2	‹1
17	Plain shoulder	1	–	‹1
18	Rustication	–	–	2

TABLE 8 Characteristics of Middle Bronze Age pottery from the Black Hole showing combinations of decorative features.

	No.	1	2	3	4	5	6	7	8	9	10	11	12	13	14	15	16	17	18	19	20	21	22	23	24	25	26	27	28	29	30	31
RIMS: Plain	1	143															18	10	1			3		7			1				1	
Finger-tipping on top	2		15																		3											
Finger-tipping on outer edge	3																															
Finger-tipping below	4																															
Finger-tipping/finger-nail on top	5																															
Finger-nail on top	6																															
Finger-nail on outer edge	7																															
Incised herringbone on top	8						2										1															
Incised opposed lines on top	9																															
Incised diagonal line on inner edge	10																															
Incised diagonal line on outer edge	11											5													1							
Incised diagonal line on top	12												62				10	2			1	1	2				3					
Incised vertical line on inner edge	13																															
Incised vertical line on outer edge	14																															
Other impressions on top	15															10	1										1					
PERFORATIONS between rim and shoulder	16																23										1					
KNOBS	17																	22	1													
COMB IMPRESSIONS	18																		16													
RUSTICATION	19																															
FINGER-NAIL IMPRESSIONS	20																				15											
LIGHT SCORING	21																					7		2								
HEAVY SCORING	22																						2									
FINGER-TIPPING ON SHOULDER	23																															
SHOULDER CORDON: with finger-tipping	24																								77							
With other impressions	25																									1						
With incised diagonal lines	26																										24					
With incised herringbone	27																											12				
Plain	28																															
FINGER-TIPPING ON INSIDE OF BASE	29																													2		
DRILL HOLES	30																														1	
BASE ANGLES	31																															20

TABLE 9 Characteristics of Middle Bronze Age pottery from Shaft X showing combinations of decorative features.
(Note 4 rim sherds carrying finger-tipping on inner and outer edge and perforations through the wall between rim and shoulder not included.)

Feature	#	1	2	3	4	5	6	7	8	9	10	11	12	13	14	15	16	17	18	19	20	21	22	23	24	25	26	27	28	29	30	31
RIMS: Plain	1	169															9	6														
Finger-tipping on top	2		56														5	5						4								
Finger-tipping on outer edge	3																															
Finger-tipping below	4				1																				1							
Finger-tipping/finger-nail on top	5					2																										
Finger-nail on top	6																															
Finger-nail on outer edge	7																															
Incised herringbone on top	8																															
Incised opposed lines on top	9																															
Incised diagonal line on inner edge	10																															
Incised diagonal line on outer edge	11											10																				
Incised diagonal line on top	12												38				3							2								
Incised vertical line on inner edge	13																															
Incised vertical line on outer edge	14																															
Other impressions on top	15															3																
PERFORATIONS between rim and shoulder	16																33															
KNOBS	17																	16														
COMB IMPRESSIONS	18																															
RUSTICATION	19																															
FINGER-NAIL IMPRESSIONS	20																															
LIGHT SCORING	21																					1										
HEAVY SCORING	22																						9									
FINGER-TIPPING ON SHOULDER	23																							12								
SHOULDER CORDON: with finger-tipping	24																								56							
With other impressions	25																									1						
With incised diagonal lines	26																										24					
With incised herringbone	27																											1				
Plain	28																												6			
FINGER-TIPPING ON INSIDE OF BASE	29																															
DRILL HOLES	30																															3
BASE ANGLES	31																															136

Density	1	‹5 fragments/sq. cm of surface	(sparse)
	2	5-10 fragments/sq. cm	(medium)
	3	›10 fragments/sq.cm	(dense)
Fragment size	S	‹0.5mm diameter	(small)
	M	0.5-1.0mm diameter	(medium)
	L	›1.0mm diameter	(large)
Filler type	F	crushed calcined flint	
	Sh	shell	
	G	grog	
	Ch	chalk	
	S	sand	
	Q	quartz	

Identification and coding of the fabrics was complicated by the fact that the occurrence and density of grog was difficult to assess by eye and, further, by the occurrence of shell and flint fragments within the grog particles as well as within the clay matrix of the fabric. The assessments of abundance expressed in the fabric codes account for the inclusions added to the clay as well as inclusions contained within any grog particles. A small sample of sherds, submitted for petrological examination, was analysed in thin section, Table 10. The thin sections showed up very small particles of flint and shell which are not visible under low magnification. Thus, there are certain discrepancies between the table of included materials visible in thin section and those assessed by eye. However, the visible inclusions are more likely to reflect the deliberately added temper, both in the matrix and within any grog inclusions, because the tempering materials would have been ground down until the largest fragments reached the size mode required by the potter. Thus, when considering coarse fabrics such as those encountered at Grimes Graves, the visual estimation of filler types is most likely to reflect the technological differences within and between contemporary assemblages.

The petrological analysis has shown that the clay used contained a variable amount of quartz-rich sand and a little rounded flint. The main deliberate inclusions were flint, shell and grog which were utilised in various densities and combinations. The occurrence of these combinations of fabric types are shown in fig. 15, where the visual fabric counts are arranged according to trait groups for the Black Hole

and Shaft X assemblages respectively. fig. 16 shows the total fabric counts for these groups and for the Oppenheimer Collection.

In all three assemblages the highest counts are for grog inclusions and grog/flint or grog/shell combinations (fig. 16). These fabric types are followed in degree of occurrence by medium flint inclusions and small and medium shell fragments. In all cases, high densities of any inclusions are very rare and the size of inclusions usually lies in the small or medium ranges. Although minor variations in fabric occur between the different trait groups (fig. 15) no significant patterns are apparent. In the Black Hole assemblage there may be some tendency for the decorated rims to have a grogged fabric, rather than gritted, and for the smaller decorated vessels, with knobs or perforations to have been made from clay filled with grog. However, among the vessels from Shaft X the occurrence of grogged fabrics is more evenly distributed through the trait groups and so this apparent distinction cannot be regarded as a general functional or stylistic characteristic.

(c) **Internal Chronology**

In the light of the variety of forms, decorative techniques and fabrics described above it is imperative to establish whether the currency of the individual traits might have altered through time. A consideration of the stratification of the two major sites is therefore of primary importance.

From the archives concerning the excavation of the Black Hole, which are held in the British Museum, it has proved possible to plot the derivation of the potsherds by 3-foot square, both in plan and on the section. This demonstrates that the pottery was evenly distributed throughout the deposit between the depths of 3 feet and 8 feet, although in plan the major concentration of pottery was found within a relatively small area approximately 6 feet in diameter. This may have been the fill of a pit, unrecognised by Armstrong. Analysis of the recorded depths for 12 sets of joining feature sherds indicated that fragments of individual vessels were dispersed throughout the excavated deposits - e.g. vessels *51* between 4 and 8 feet, vessel *133* between 1 and 5 feet and vessel *245* from 4 to 7 feet depths.

A similar study was undertaken for the contexts of the large ceramic assemblage from Shaft X whereby the occurrence of sherds displaying particular traits was investigated in relation to the disposition of the three main midden deposits. This showed that all the main ceramic traits: 1, 2, 4, 5, 10, 13 and 15, were represented in all three midden deposits. No sherds with applied knobs (trait 7) were found in Midden I and none with perforations (trait 3) in Midden III. Traits, 8, 11 and 16 occurred only in midden deposit II, but these layers produced many more diagnostic sherds (53) than middens I or III, both with 32 feature sherds. The remarkable homogeneity of the three main pottery-bearing deposits is well in accord with the hypothesis that the whole of phase II may only have lasted between two and ten years. Although the records relating to the contexts for the Black Hole pottery are rather more ambiguous, the analyses noted above suggest that the deposit there also represented a single event, namely the infilling of the top of a shaft, or of a pit dug within it, with a dump of refuse rich in domestic debris but lacking any meaningful internal stratification.

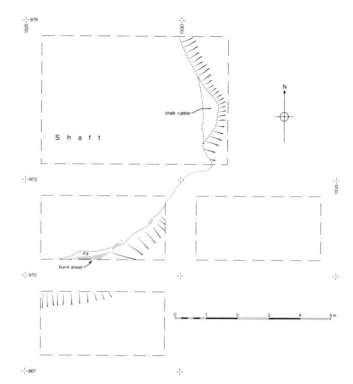

fig. 14   Plan of Cuttings 1325.5/967.5, 1325.5/970.5, 1325.5/973.5 and 1330.5/910.5, Area C.

TABLE 10   Petrographic features of Middle Bronze Age sherds revealed by thin section

Sherd Cat. No.	SAND			SILT	FLINT IN SAND	CHALK	FLINT TEMPER	GROG	SHELL IN GROG	FLINT IN GROG	SHELL
	Coarse >.5mm	Medium 0.5-0.25	Fine 0.25-0.06	0.06>							
3	-	3	3	3	?1	3	?3	5	1	-	4
4	2	2	3	3	-	3	4	4	-	1	-
49	2	3	3	3	-	-	4/5	4	1	-	3
60	-	3	3	3	-	-	5	4	1	-	3
73	-	3	3	3	-	-	2	4	1	-	3
138	2	3	4	4	-	4	-	4	1	-	4
150	3	4	4	4	1	3	3	4	1	1	4
230	2	3	3	3	-	-	-	4	1	-	4
236	-	2	3	3	-	-	5	-	-	-	5
247	-	3	3	4	1	-	3	3	1	-	4
251	2	3	3	3	1	-	?3	4	1	-	4
252	-	3	3	3	1	-	?2	?3	?	-	3
258	3	3	3	3	1	-	-	4	1	1	4
310	-	2	3	3	-	-	5	?3	-	?1	-
311	3	4	3	3	1	-	-	4	-	-	3
389	3	4	4/5	4	1	-	-	-	-	-	4/5
407	-	3	4	4	-	-	-	4	1	-	4
410	-	2	3	3	-	-	5	-	-	-	-
433	3	4	4	4	-	-	-	-	-	-	4
469	-	4	4	3	-	-	-	5	1	-	4

-	Absent	3	Sparse/occasional
1	Present (in variable amounts)	4	Common
2	Present, rare	5	Abundant

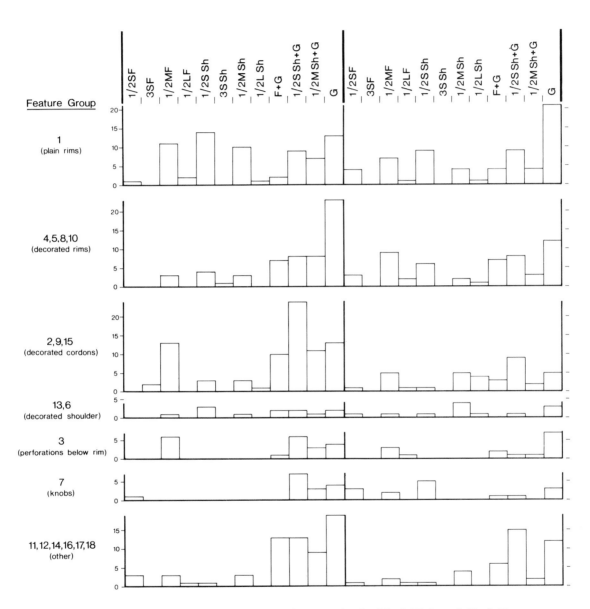

fig. 15   Occurrence of fabrics by trait group in the Black Hole and Shaft X.

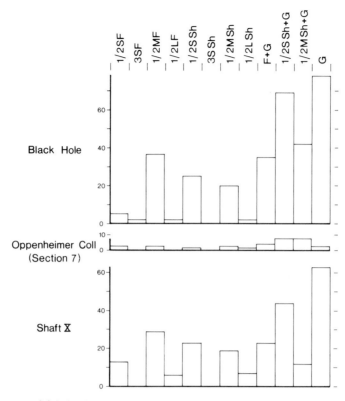

fig. 16   Occurrence of fabrics in the Black Hole, Shaft X and Section 7 (Oppenheimer Coll.).

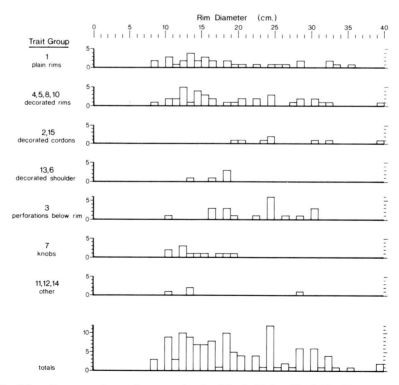

fig. 17   Rim diameters by trait group in the Black Hole, Shaft X, Mercer's 1971/2
Excavation and Section 7 (Oppenheimer Coll.).

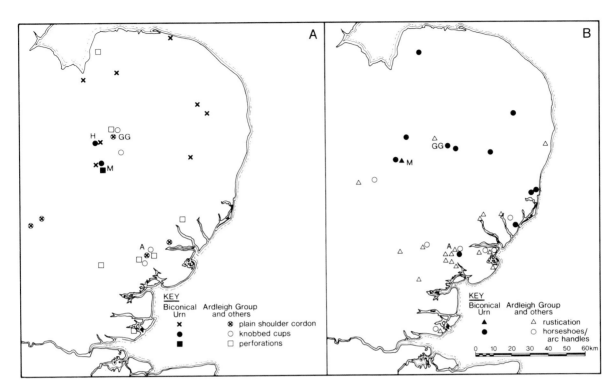

fig. 18   The distribution of selected decorative motifs in East Anglia. GG:
Grimes Graves; H: Hockwold; M: Mildenhall Fen; A: Ardleigh.

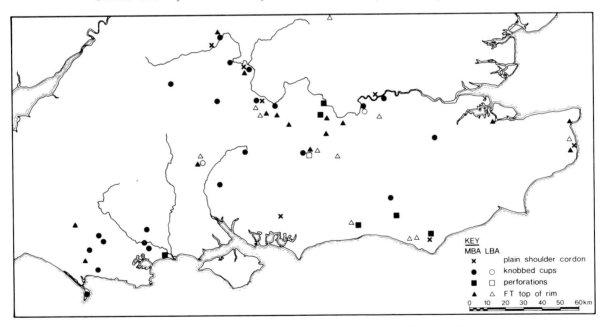

fig. 19   The distribution of selected characteristics in Southern England.

(d) Functional Groups

In recent years it has become customary to view prehistoric ceramics in terms of their proposed functions within the social and economic environment. Thus, the process of stylistic change and the variations in vessel size and degree of adornment may be related to overall trends in social behaviour and economic development. The contrast between the size and shape of Middle Bronze Age vessel categories and those of the Late Bronze Age has been studied by Barrett (1980: figs. 2 and 3). In part he was able to measure the volumes relating to complete vessels but for other sections of the analysis, where the material to be assessed was more fragmentary in nature, the diameter of the vessel mouth was used as a measure of vessel size. Other methods include the employment of rim diameter/vessel height ratios (Ellison 1975) and, in the case of extremely fragmented material, the measurement of sherd thickness (Ellison 1982). Using these techniques a three-fold functional division of Middle Bronze Age ceramics has been proposed (Ellison 1981). The heavy duty storage jars and everyday cooking pots of medium size can readily be separated from the smaller, more carefully executed, and often decorated, jars and cups which were probably employed at table.

It is instructive to examine the ceramic assemblage from Grimes Graves according to these principles and, in order to do so, an extensive study of rim diameters, base diameters and sherd thickness was undertaken. A clear relationship between base diameters and body wall thickness was established, but that between rim diameter and wall thickness was more variable (data in archive). The range in vessel size is best illustrated by the range of rim diameters, summarised in fig. 17. The distribution of all measurable rim diameters, from the four main collections: Black Hole, Shaft X, Section 7 (Oppenheimer Coll.) and Mercer 1971/72 is shown at the base of fig. 17. The histogram shows two main peaks, in the ranges 10 to 18cm and 28 to 31cm respectively, and the sharp peak at 24cm may represent a further size group. A similar three-fold division is shown by the distribution of base diameters. The breakdown of distribution of rim diameters within the major trait groups, also shown in fig. 17, provides further useful indications.

Vessels of all sizes are equally likely to have been provided with plain rims or rims decorated with finger-impressed or incised line ornamentation. However, decorated cordons seem to be limited to vessels in the higher size range while smaller pots were provided with a row of finger-tip impressions applied directly to the body of the vessel. The cups or jars bearing applied knobs occur only in small sizes, and the vessels supplied with a row of perforations below the rim have a fairly restricted rim diameter range, mainly between 15 and 30cm. The marked peak at 24cm forms a major component of the 24cm peak in the combined histogram below and this may indicate that the vessels with perforations were a specialised medium-sized form, expressly designed for a particular purpose.

The assemblage therefore can be broken down into three groups, defined primarily by their size characteristics, which probably performed different functions within the sites from which they originally derived.

Group	Size	Types
1	Small	knobbed cups
		small buckets with FT row at shoulder
2	medium	row of perforations
3	medium to large	large buckets decorated cordons

In the total absence of information concerning the exact location, size, structural components and layout of the site or sites from which the Grimes Graves pottery assemblages originally derive, further analyses designed to consider the spatial variation of types within and between structures cannot be attempted. Further interpretation of function therefore must rest upon comparisons drawn with data from sites elsewhere in the country.

(e) Parallels in East Anglia and Beyond

All the decorative techniques used in the Grimes Graves assemblages can be matched elsewhere in East Anglia. Their occurrences are summarised in Appendix I which lists all identifiable finds of later Bronze Age pottery in East Anglia which are known to the author. Biconical urns, recently analysed and discussed by Tomalin (1983), are listed separately from the Ardleigh Group finds and other later Bronze Age pottery from the region. The occurrence of selected traits are shown in the distribution maps figs. 18 and 19, with the sites shown on fig. 19 being listed in Appendix II.

Most traits occur in all the main typological groups

with the notable exception of cord-impressed decoration which is found only on vessels of the Biconical class. Comb-point decoration, linear incisions and finger-tip rustication are rare traits within the Grimes Graves assemblages (Tables 5 to 7). The latter is common amongst the Ardleigh Group whilst the comb and line techniques are found on various Biconical Urns in East Anglia, and beyond. However, applied horseshoe and arc handles are found in both groups and are distributed widely throughout the region (fig. 18B). Finger-tip treatment of the rim and applied shoulder cordons are very common East Anglian features and plain shoulder cordons also display a regional distribution (fig. 18A). On the other hand, the shoulder cordons and rims decorated with diagonal slashes, which form such a distinctive component of the Grimes Graves assemblages can be matched only at Ardleigh Ring III within the region, with the only other good parallel occurring at Fengate (Cambs.). Rows of perforations below the rim and applied knobs are found on several other sites in East Anglia and their distribution is also shown in fig. 18A.

Some of these traits occur commonly within later Bronze Age Deverel-Rimbury assemblages throughout southern England. However, others are found only in East Anglia or have a limited distribution extending to south-east England only (fig. 19). Thus plain shoulder cordons and finger-tip treatment of the top of the rim are found in the Thames Valley and sporadically in Kent and Sussex. Rows of perforations occur in Sussex, the Thames Valley and at Latch Farm (Hants). Knobbed cups, in contrast, are concentrated in the Thames Valley, Wiltshire and Dorset and are largely absent from south-east England. Taken as a whole, the Grimes Graves and East Anglian assemblages show most distinct affinity with those of the Thames Valley and it is instructive to note that in both these areas typological links with the local vessels belonging to the Biconical series are very marked.

The wide range of fabrics identified at Grimes Graves cannot be matched easily at any other site, either within East Anglia or beyond. Where the filler types for East Anglian vessels and assemblages have been identified they are indicated in Appendix I. Biconical Urns are usually characterised by grogged fabrics and grog also occurs in later assemblages in Norfolk, Suffolk and Lincolnshire (see Appendix I). In the latter cases, the grog is usually accompanied by flint inclusions, a combination commonly observed at Grimes Graves, while the main assemblages of the Ardleigh Group are characterised by heavy flint fillers. The shell filler which occurs fairly commonly at Grimes Graves is, however, a rarity in East Anglia, where it can be matched only by one sherd at Fengate, though it does occur in the Thames Valley and Dorset (Ellison 1975).

The percentages of various filler types represented in a selection of Bronze Age sites from East Anglia and southern England which have been subjected to detailed analysis are shown in fig. 20. The histograms have been compiled using data presented in Tomalin 1983 (356-391 for Hockwold and Shearplace Hill), Dacre and Ellison 1981 (Kimpton) and White 1982 (Simons Ground). All five sites display a wide variety of filler types but, in most cases, one type or level of density is predominant. Thus in the Hockwold (Norfolk) and Shearplace Hill (Dorset) domestic Biconical Urn assemblages grog is the most common filling agent, while at the Kimpton (Hants) Deverel-Rimbury cemetery medium and large flint inclusions predominate. At the other Deverel-Rimbury cemetery site, Simons Ground (Dorset), grog is present to a significant degree, but small flint inclusions are the most common ingredient. Whilst some regional patterning of fabric types can be detected in the later Bronze Age (Ellison 1975) the most significant aspect of recent fabric studies is the exclusiveness of the fabric range displayed at individual sites. This suggests that analyses of deliberately added inclusions are indeed beginning to contribute to the identification of the work of individual potters or potting communities in the later Bronze Age. As such research progresses, comparison with the results of Tomalin's analysis of specific grog recipes within Biconical Urn assemblages could prove to be most informative.

(f) Origins and Chronology

It has been shown that all the forms and traits found within the Grimes Graves assemblages may be paralleled in the local East Anglian Biconical Urn or Ardleigh Group traditions. The origins of the Biconical tradition have been demonstrated by Tomalin (1983) to include a series of remarkable innovations originating from Continental sources amalgamated with aspects of the Early Bronze Age urn series including Food Vessels and Collared Urns. Food Vessel Urns in East Anglia are very rare but Collared Urns are fairly densely and evenly distributed (Longworth 1984, fig. 42). The few available radiocarbon dates would suggest that Biconical Urns may have been current from the 16th to the 12th centuries bc. Vessels of the Ardleigh Group, like those belonging to the South Lodge Type of Barrel Urns, display various decorative motifs which involve skeuomorphic imagery of the rope cordon, arc handle and carrying-net. As Tomalin has shown, this imagery forms one of the definitive characteristics of the Biconical series. It has been argued elsewhere that a late Early Bronze Age/early Middle Bronze Age date should be advanced for the Barrel Urns with plastic decoration (Dacre and Ellison 1981, 192) and it is proposed that a similarly early date should apply to the Ardleigh Group assemblages. The single date of 1335 ± 85bc (1680-1500, 1475-1460 BC Calibrated) from Barling (Essex) (BM-1631) might assist such an hypothesis, though that of 825 ± 35 bc (985-900 BC Calibrated) from Braintree (Essex) (BM-1632) might also suggest a lengthy currency for the type. More persuasive perhaps is the relative distribution of Biconical Urns and Ardleigh Group vessels in East Anglia (see fig. 18B). Biconicals are located mainly in Norfolk whilst the Ardleigh urns display a tight distribution in Suffolk and Essex which has long been demonstrated (Erith and Longworth 1960, fig. 8). These complementary distributions suggest that the two types may have been in use contemporaneously with both current during the later Early Bronze Age period.

In southern East Anglia the Ardleigh tradition seems to have persisted, with the gradual introduction of certain new traits such as rows of perforations below the rim (Couchman 1975), until the development of the distinctive Late Bronze Age assemblages identified and dated at such sites as Mucking and Orsett, both in Essex (Jones and Bond 1980; Barrett in Hedges and Buckley 1978). However, in Norfolk the strong Biconical tradition appears to have given way to the less ornately decorated but still diverse ceramic styles that are so well exemplified in the assemblages from Grimes Graves. The extensive series of radiocarbon dates from the site indicate that the Bronze Age occupation is likely to fall within the bracket c1050-850 bc (Calibrated 1375-845 BC) (Burleigh et al 1979, 46). This would align the tradition chronologically with the later stages of the southern Deverel-Rimbury tradition and the Post Deverel-Rimbury phase as defined by Barrett (1980). By the 6th century BC it was superseded by the West Harling and Fengate-Cromer styles as defined by Cunliffe (1974, figs. 3.2 and 3.4).

Of the more specific and diagnostic traits recognised in the Grimes Graves assemblage some detailed discussion is required. Comb-point decoration occurs rarely within the Ardleigh Group, both at Ardleigh itself (Erith and Longworth 1960: Urn C2 and Urn fig 4a) as well as at White Colne. Comb-point and incised line decoration both occur at Mildenhall Fen (Grimes Graves *247* cf. Clark 1936 fig. 5, 8 and 14; Grimes Graves *513* cf. Clark 1936 fig. 8). The incised motifs represented at Grimes Graves cannot be reconstructed but those at Mildenhall Fen, characteristic of the 'Mildenhall Ware' defined by Clark include cross-hatched lozenges and triangles which are reminiscent of certain motifs found in the Ardleigh Group repertoire and both groups of decoration can be matched most easily amongst the later Beaker pottery of the region. Relevant examples would include Southern Handled Beakers from Risby Warren (Lincs), Gresham and North Creake (Norfolk) and March (Cambs) (Clarke 1970, corpus nos. 1080, 1076, 1070, 1055) and sherds from the domestic assemblages at Hockwold (eg Bamford 1982, figs. 2,3,4 and 19). The finger-tip impressed top of rim and plain shoulder cordons have been noted as traits which occur only rarely outside East Anglia in the Middle and Late Bronze Age but both were fairly common within the Biconical tradition as a whole. Thus plain cordons occur on 44 examples of Biconical Urns listed by Tomalin and finger-tipped rims on nine examples, both with distributions extending from Dorset to Lincolnshire and Yorkshire. The shallow-necked rim profile occurs on four Biconical Urns, including that from Stonea (Cambs), and although only occurring in the Black Hole assemblage, this trait appears to have been a component of the style from the beginning. Rows of perforations below the rim and knobs are not found in the Biconical tradition. These are primarily functional traits concerned with the attachment of presumably organic lids and covers. They can therefore be viewed as a replacement, and indeed simplification, of the complex types of collar and lugs employed for cover attachment in the Early Bronze Age.

(g) Functional Diversity

It has been demonstrated above that the Grimes Graves assemblages, taken individually and as a whole, may be broken down into three ceramic groups based on size and it was suggested that these groups were designed to perform varying functions within the domestic environment. It is now appropriate to contrast these results with comparable data acquired from other later Bronze Age sites and fig. 21 plots this data for 11 other sites located in East Anglia or southern England. The sources of data used in figs. 21 and 22 are listed in Appendix III. It can be seen that, although few of these other assemblages approach that from Grimes Graves in size, the histograms often display peaks which may be of functional relevance. When these apparent peaks are emphasised and the assemblages are arranged in a putative chronological order some interesting patterns emerge (fig. 22). An overall consideration of size ranges shows that a trend towards very large vessels was initiated during the currency of Biconical Urns and lasted through the life of relief-decorated urns in East Anglia and the south. Following the demise of complex plastic decoration sizes were reduced once more and size peaks approximated more closely to those of Early Bronze Age times, although the overall size *ranges* were reduced. The exact function of the very large urns of the final Early Bronze Age and early Middle Bronze Age cannot be proven but storage in the absence of domestic pits seems a possible theory; what is more certain is that their introduction probably related to the influx of European pots or potters postulated by Tomalin (1983).

The other major pattern to emerge from fig. 22 is that the number of size peaks shows a general increase from two (smaller and larger) to a consistent three (small, medium and large) by the developed Middle Bronze Age. This may be viewed as the early stages of the phenomenon of type diversification described for the Late Bronze Age by Barrett (1980). Similar patterns occur throughout within domestic and sepulchral assemblages and, on the present evidence, it would seem that vessels for burials were selected from the current domestic pottery repertoires. However, further detailed evidence from more sites might cause such a simplistic hypothesis to be modified.

In comparison with assemblages of a similar phase, the Grimes Graves ceramic size array seems to be fairly typical and it could be postulated that the assemblage derived from a domestic settlement of standard later Bronze Age type. It would be tempting to link the relatively high value of the largest size peak to a preponderance of super-heavyduty vessels which might be associated functionally with the dairying economy postulated from analysis of faunal remains

from the deposits (Legge *et. al.* forthcoming), but the overall lack of comparative data does not allow such detailed deduction at the present time. The high incidence of traits associated with the provision of tight lids and covers - the rows of perforations and knobs - certainly would be consistent with the use of vessels for the storage and processing of delicate dairy products subject to contamination and rapid decomposition. Only the preparation of further analyses similar to those presented in this discussion can lead to the elucidation of such enquiries and it is hoped that the present study may stimulate their conception.

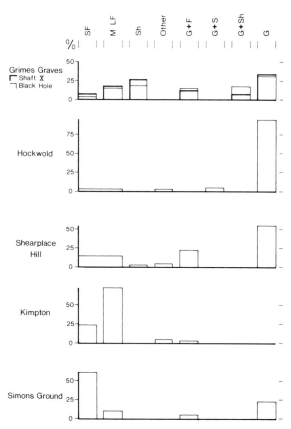

fig. 20   The occurrence of filler types in selected Bronze Age ceramic assemblages.

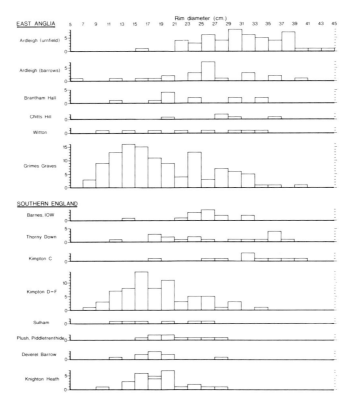

fig. 21   The distribution of rim diameters in selected later Bronze Age assemblages.

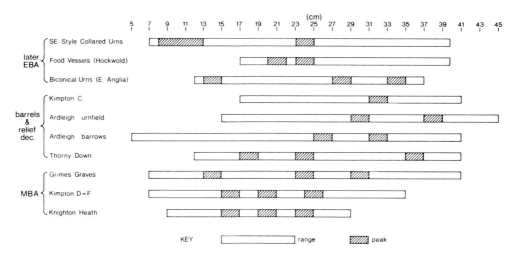

fig. 22   The distribution of rim size ranges in selected Bronze Age assemblages.

Illustrated Catalogue

ARMSTRONG COLLECTION: 'Black hole'

1 14 undecorated sherds including rim, 2 joining, and base. Light brown both faces with grey core. Fabric: 2 M F. Rim diam. 26cm.
5, 5F5, 6, 7F2, 'Kit. Site'

2 Undecorated rim sherd. Light brown to grey both faces, with grey core. Fabric: 2 S Sh.
-

3 6 undecorated sherds including rim, 3 joining. Light brown to grey both faces. Fabric: 2 G. Rim diam. 13 cm.
7E3, 3F5, 4F1A, 7D3, 8D4

4 2 undecorated rim sherds. Light grey to brown both faces, dark grey core. Fabric: 2 S Sh. Rim diam. 20 cm.
4FIA, 7

5 Undecorated rim sherd. Light brown both faces with dark grey core. Fabric: 2 S Sh; 1 L Sh. Rim diam. 24 cm.
5B6

6 Undecorated rim sherd. Light brown throughout. Fabric: 1 M Sh; G. Rim diam. 14 cm.
5F5

7 2 undecorated rim sherds. Light brown externally, light brown to brown internally, with grey core. Fabric: 1 S Sh; 1 G.
-

8 Undecorated rim sherd. Grey both faces. Fabric: - .Rim diam. 15cm.
-

9 Undecorated rim sherd. Light brown throughout. Fabric: 2 S Sh; G.
5C6

10 Undecorated rim sherd. Light brown both faces with grey core. Fabric: 1 S F; 1 S Sh.
4

11 Undecorated rim sherd. Light brown both faces with grey core. Fabric: 1 S Sh; G.
-

12 Undecorated rim sherd. Light brown externally, grey internally. Fabric: 1 M Sh.
-

13 Undecorated rim sherd. Grey to brown externally, brown internally. Fabric. 1 M Sh; G.
-

14 Undecorated rim sherd. Grey to brown both faces. Fabric: 2 M F; 1 G. Rim diam. 15 cm.
-

15 Undecorated rim sherd. Light brown to grey externally, light brown internally, with dark grey core. Fabric: 1 S Sh.
C7

16 Undecorated rim sherd. Light brown externally, grey to light brown internally. Fabric: 2 L Sh.
-

17 Undecorated rim sherd. Brown to grey externally, grey internally. Fabric: M G; (specks of Sh).
5F3

18 Undecorated rim sherd. Grey to brown both faces, with grey core. Fabric: 1 S Sh.
G54

19 Undecorated rim sherd. Light brown externally, light brown to grey internally with grey core. Fabric: 1 S Sh; 1 L Sh.
-

20 Undecorated rim sherd. Light brown externally, grey internally. Fabric: 1 S Sh; G.
-

21 Undecorated rim sherd. Light brown both faces with grey core. 2 M Sh; G. Rim diam. 28 cm.
-

22 Undecorated rim sherd. Light brown both faces, with grey core, surface eroded internally. Fabric: 2 M G.
-

23 Undecorated rim sherd. Reddish brown externally, reddish brown to grey internally with grey core. Fabric: 1 S; G.
4E3

24 Undecorated rim sherd. Grey externally, light brown to grey internally. Fabric: 1 S Sh.
-

25 Undecorated rim sherd. Light brown to grey externally, grey internally. Fabric: 2 M G.
-

26 Undecorated rim sherd. Grey to brown externally, light brown internally. Fabric: 2 L F.
5F3

27 Undecorated rim sherd. Grey throughout. Fabric: 1 M G; 1 M Sh.
-

28 Undecorated rim sherd. Light brown externally, grey internally, with dark grey core. Fabric: 1 G.
-

29 Undecorated rim sherd. Light brown both faces. Fabric: 1 M Sh. Rim diam. 10 cm.
-

30 Undecorated rim sherd. Light brown externally, light brown to grey internally. Fabric: 1 S Sh; G. Rim diam. 10 cm.
-

31 Undecorated rim sherd. Grey to brown externally, grey internally. Fabric: 1 S Sh; 1 L G.
-

32 Undecorated rim sherd. Grey both faces. Fabric: G.
-

33 Undecorated rim sherd. Patchy grey to brown externally, grey internally. Fabric: 1 G.
-

34 Undecorated rim sherd. Grey externally. Internal surface eroded. Fabric: 2 S Sh.
-

35 Undercorated rim sherd. Light brown both faces with dark grey core. Fabric: 2 M G.
FIA

36 Undecorated rim sherd. Grey to brown both faces. Fabric: 1 L F. Rim diam. 8 cm.
8C3

37 Undecorated rim sherd. Grey throughout. Fabric: 2 G. Rim diam. 11 cm.
7D4

38 Undecorated rim sherd. Reddish brown both faces with grey core. Fabric: 1 S Sh.
'Kit. Site'

39 Undecorated rim sherd. Brown both faces with grey core. Fabric: 1 S F; 1 S Sh.
-

40 Undecorated rim sherd. Brown both faces. Fabric: 2 M F.
-

41 3 undecorated rim sherds and 1 wall, joining. Grey to light brown externally, grey internally. Fabric: 1 M F. Rim diam. 16 cm.
5, 5F2

42 Undecorated rim sherd. Light brown externally, brown to grey internally, with grey core. Fabric: 2 S Sh. Rim diam. 18 cm.
-

43 Undecorated rim sherd. Grey to brown externally, grey internally. Fabric: 1 M F; 1 M Sh.
5C8

44 Undecorated rim sherd. Brown externally, grey internally. Fabric: 1 M F; 1 S Sh.

45 2 undecorated rim sherds and 1 wall, joining, of well fired paste tempered with a little grit, grey throughout. External surface irregular but well smoothed.
5E2

46 Undecorated rim sherd. Grey externally, grey to brown internally. Fabric: M G.
5

47 Undecorated rim sherd. Grey externally, grey to light brown internally. Fabric: 1 M F. Rim diam. 13 cm.
-

48 Undecorated rim sherd. Light brown both faces. Fabric: 1 S Sh; G.
-

49 3 undecorated rim sherds. Light brown to grey both faces. Fabric: 1 M F.
5, 5F2

50 Undecorated rim sherd. Light brown externally, brown to dark grey internally. Fabric: 1 M Sh.
-

51 Undecorated rim to base sherd. Patchy grey to brown both faces. Fabric: 1 G. Rim diam. 8 cm.
8E4

52 Undecorated rim sherd. Light brown both faces. Fabric: 1 M Sh.
-

53 2 undecorated rim sherds, joining. Grey externally, grey to brown internally. Fabric: 2 M Sh; 1 L Sh; G. Rim diam. 28 cm.
5E4, 5F1

54 Undecorated rim sherd. Grey throughout. Fabric: 1 S Sh; 1 G. Rim diam. 14 cm.
8F4

55 Undecorated rim sherd. Brown externally, brown to grey internally with dark grey core. Fabric: 1 S Sh.
-

56 Undecorated rim sherd. Light brown both faces. Fabric: 1 M Sh; 2 M G.
-

57 Undecorated rim sherd. Light brown throughout. Fabric: 2 S Sh; 1 M G.
-

58 Undecorated rim sherd. Light brown externally, brown internally. Fabric: 1 G; 1 S F.
-

59 Undecorated rim sherd. Grey throughout. Fabric: M G.
-

60 4 undecorated rim sherds (3 joining) and 1 base angle. Light brown to grey both faces, with dark grey core. Fabric: 1 S Sh. Rim diam. 10 cm.
5E4

61 Undecorated rim sherd. Grey to light brown both faces with grey core. Fabric: 1 S Sh.
1G3

62 Undecorated rim sherd. Grey externally, grey to brown internally. Fabric: 1 S Sh; G.
5

63 6 undecorated rim sherds, 3 joining. Brown to grey both faces with dark grey core. Fabric: 2 M F. Rim diam. 25 cm.
7C4, 8D4

64 Undecorated rim sherd. Brown both faces with dark grey core. Fabric: 2 M Sh.
-

65 Undecorated rim sherd. Brown externally, brown to grey internally with grey core. Fabric: 1 M Sh.
7D4

66 11 undecorated sherds, 3 joining. Light brown to grey both faces. External surface roughly smoothed. Fabric: 1 M F; 2 M Sh; 1 L Sh. Rim diam. 32 cm.
4FIA, 5F2, 6E3, 7C3, 7F3, 8E4

67 Undecorated rim sherd. Light brown both faces, with grey core. Fabric: 1 M Sh. Rim diam. 12 cm.
-

68   Undecorated rim sherd. Grey to brown externally, light brown internally. Fabric: 1 M Sh; G.

-

69   Undecorated rim sherd. Grey externally, grey to brown internally. Fabric: 1 M Sh.

-

70   Undecorated rim sherd. Light brown externally, light brown to grey internally, with grey core. Fabric: 2 M Sh; G.

-

71   Undecorated rim sherd. Grey throughout. Fabric: 1 M Sh; G.

-

72   Undecorated rim sherd. Light brown both faces with grey core. Fabric: 1 S Sh; some G.

-

73   2 rim sherds, joining. Light brown to grey both faces. Decoration: On the shoulder cordon, a row of finger tip impressions. Fabric: 3 M G. Rim diam. 20 cm.
5F3

74   2 joining wall sherds. Light brown to grey externally, internal surface lost. Decoration: On the shoulder cordon, finger tip impressions. Fabric: 2 M Sh; 2 L G.
7F3

75   Wall sherd. Light brown both faces with grey core. Decoration: On the shoulder cordon, finger tip impressions. Fabric: 1 S Sh; 2 M G.
7F4

76   Rim and wall sherds, joining. Brown to grey externally, grey to light brown internally. Decoration: On the external edge of the rim, diag. incisions. On the shoulder cordon, a row of finger tip impressions. Fabric: 1 S Sh; 2 L G. Rim diam. 32 cm.

-

77   Wall sherd. Light brown externally, brown internally. Decoration: On the shoulder cordon, ? finger tip impressions. Fabric: 2 M G.

-

78   Wall sherd. Light brown to grey externally, grey to brown internally. Decoration: On the shoulder cordon, a row of finger tip impressions. Fabric: 2 L G.
5

79   Rim Sherd. Light brown to grey both faces. Decoration: On the shoulder cordon a row of finger tip impressions. Fabric: 2 M F; 1 L F. Rim diam. 30 cm.

-

80   Wall sherd. Light brown externally, light brown to grey internally, with grey core. Decoration: On the shoulder cordon, a row of finger tip impressions. Fabric: 3 S F.
41A

81   2 joining wall sherds. Light brown externally, brown internally. Decoration: On the shoulder cordon, diagonal finger tip impressions. Fabric: 1 S Sh; 2 M G.
4F(?)

82   Wall sherd. Brown both faces. Decoration: On the shoulder cordon, a row of finger tip impressions. Fabric: 1 S Sh; 1 M G.
F55

83   2 wall sherds, joining. Light brown to grey both faces. Decoration: On the shoulder cordon, a row of finger tip impressions. Fabric: 1 S Sh; 1 M G.
5E2, 8D4

84   Wall sherd. Brown both faces. Decoration: On the shoulder cordon, a row of finger tip impressions. Fabric: 1 S Sh; 2 M G.
G34

85   Wall sherd. Light brown to brown externally, grey internally. Decoration: On the shoulder cordon, a row of finger tip impressions. Fabric: 2 M Sh.

-

86   Wall sherd. Grey both faces. Decoration: On the shoulder cordon, a row of ?finger tip impressions. Fabric: 1 M F; 1 M G.

-

87   Wall sherd. Light brown externally, grey internally. Decoration: On the shoulder cordon, a row of finger tip impressions. Fabric: 1 S Sh.
8F4

88   Wall sherd: Grey both faces. Decoration: On the shoulder cordon, a row of finger tip impressions. Fabric: 1 M F; 2 M G.
-

89   Wall sherd. Light brown both faces. Decoration: On the shoulder cordon, a row of finger tip impressions. Fabric: 1 M F.
'Kit. Site'

90   Wall sherd. Brown both faces. Decoration: On the shoulder cordon, a row of finger tip impressions. Fabric: 1 M F.
-

91   Wall sherd. Light brown to grey both faces. Decoration: On the shoulder cordon, a row of finger tip impressions. Fabric: 3 S F; 1 L F.
6

92   Wall sherd. Light brown to grey both faces. Decoration: On the shoulder cordon, a finger tip impression. Fabric: 1 M Sh.
-

93   Wall sherd. Light brown to grey externally, grey internally. Decoration: On the shoulder cordon, a row of ?finger tip impressions. Fabric: 1 M F; 1 S Sh.
-

94   Wall sherd. Brown externally, brown to grey internally. Decoration: On the shoulder cordon, a row of finger tip impressions. Fabric: 1 M Sh; 1 L G.
-

95   Wall sherd. Brown both faces. Decoration: On the shoulder cordon, remains of a row of finger tip impressions. Fabric: 1 S Sh; G.
-

96   Wall sherd. Grey both faces. Decoration: On the shoulder cordon, a row of finger tip impressions. Fabric: ?
-

97   Wall sherd. Light brown to grey externally, grey internally. Decoration: On the shoulder cordon, a row of finger tip impressions. Fabric: 1 M Sh; G.
-

98   Wall sherd. Light brown both faces with grey core. Decoration: On the shoulder cordon, a row of finger tip impressions. Two finger nail impressions beneath on the body. Fabric: 2 S Sh.
-

99   Wall sherd. Light brown externally, grey to brown internally. Decoration: On the shoulder cordon, a row of finger tip impressions. Fabric: 1 S Sh; G.
-

100   Wall sherd. Light brown externally, grey to light brown internally. Decoration: On the shoulder cordon, a row of finger tip impressions. Fabric: 2 M F; 1 L F
4F2

101   Wall sherd. Brown externally, grey internally. Decoration: on the shoulder cordon, a row of finger tip impressions. Fabric: 2 S Sh.
-

102   Wall sherd. Light brown to grey both faces. Decoration: On the shoulder cordon, a row of finger tip impressions. Fabric: 1 S Sh; 1 L G.
-

103   Wall sherd. Light brown both faces. Decoration: On the shoulder cordon, a row of ?finger tip impressions. Fabric: 2 M Sh; 1 L F; 1 LG.
3G5

104   2 wall sherds, joining. Light brown externally, brown internally with grey core. Decoration: On the shoulder cordon, a row of diagonal finger tip impressions. Fabric: 1 L G.
-

105   Wall sherd. Light brown to grey externally, internal surface lost. Decoration: On the shoulder cordon, a row of finger tip impressions. Fabric: 1 L Sh; G.
6F3

106   Wall sherd. Light brown externally, grey internally. Decoration: On the shoulder cordon, a row of finger tip impressions: Fabric: 2 L Sh.
7

107   Wall sherd. Grey to light brown both faces. Decoration: On the shoulder cordon, a row of diagonal finger tip impressions. Fabric: 1 L G.
5F2

108 Wall sherd. Brown both faces with dark grey core. Decoration: Remains of shoulder cordon with finger tip impression. Fabric: 1 L G

-

109 Wall sherd. Light brown both faces. Decoration: On the shoulder cordon, a row of finger tip impressions. Fabric: 2 M Sh; 2 M G.

-

110 Wall sherd. Brown both faces with dark grey core. Decoration: On the shoulder cordon, a row of finger tip impressions. Fabric: 1 M F.

-

111 Wall sherd. Light brown both faces. Decoration: On the shoulder cordon, a row of finger tip impressions. Fabric: 1 S Sh; G.

-

112 Wall sherd. Brown both faces. Decoration: On the shoulder cordon, remains of finger tip impressions. Fabric: 1 S Sh; G.
5

113 Wall sherd. Light brown externally, internal surface mainly lost. Decoration: On the shoulder cordon, a finger tip impression. Fabric: 1 S Sh; G.
5F2

114 Wall sherd. Light brown externally, brown internally. Decoration: On the shoulder cordon, a finger tip impression. Fabric: 2 M G.
5D4

115 Wall sherd. Brown both faces. Decoration: On the shoulder cordon, a row of finger tip impressions. Fabric: 1 M F.

-

116 Wall sherd. Light brown to grey externally, brown internally. Decoration: On the shoulder cordon, a row of finger tip impressions. Fabric: 1 M F.
8E4

117 Wall sherd. Light brown both faces with dark grey core. Decoration: On the shoulder cordon, a row of finger tip impressions. Fabric: 1 S Sh; 2 L G.

-

118 Wall sherd. Brown externally, brownish grey internally. Decoration: On the shoulder cordon, a row of finger tip impressions. Fabric: 1 M F.

-

119 Wall sherd. Light brown both faces with grey core. Decoration: On the shoulder cordon, a finger tip impression. Fabric: 1 S Sh; 2 LG.

-

120 Wall sherd. Light brown externally, internal surface lost. Decoration: On the shoulder cordon, a finger tip impression. Fabric: 1 M F; G.

-

121 Shoulder cordon, light brown externally. Decoration: A row of finger tip impressions. Fabric: 1 M Sh; G.

-

122 2 fragments of shoulder cordon, joining. Light brown externally. Decoration: Finger tip impressions. Fabric: 1 M F.

-

123 Wall sherd. Light brown externally, grey internally. Decoration: On the shoulder cordon, remains of a finger tip impression. Fabric: 2 L G.

-

124 Wall sherd. Brown externally, internal surface lost. Decoration: On the shoulder cordon, a row of finger tip impressions. Fabric: 1 S Sh; G.

-

125 Wall sherd. Light brown externally, internal surface lost. Decoration: On the shoulder cordon, a row of finger tip impressions. Fabric: 2 M F.
5D7

126 Wall sherd. Grey both faces with grey core. Decoration: On the shoulder cordon, remains of a finger tip impression. Fabric: 2 M Sh.

-

127 Wall sherd. Light brown externally, internal surface lost. Decoration: On the shoulder cordon, a row of finger tip impressions. Fabric: 1 S Sh; G.
E55

128 Wall sherd. Light brown both faces. Decoration: On the shoulder cordon, remains of finger tip impressions. Fabric: 1 M F.

-

129 3 undecorated rim sherds, 2 joining. Grey both faces. A row of perforations made before firing set beneath the rim.
Fabric: 1 M Sh; 1 L G. Rim diam. 24 cm.
1G3, 5F4

130 Wall sherd. Light brown externally, grey internally . Decoration: On the shoulder, a row of finger tip impressions. Fabric: 1 S Sh; G.
-

130a Wall sherd. Reddish brown both faces. Decoration: On the shoulder cordon, a finger tip impression. Fabric: 1 S Sh; G (not illustrated).
-

131 Two undecorated rim sherds, joining. Light brown both faces. A row of perforations made before firing set beneath the rim. Fabric: 2 M G. Rim diam. 18cm.
5C6½

132 Undecorated rim sherd. Grey externally, light brown to grey internally. A row of perforations made before firing set beneath the rim. Fabric: 2 M F.
7

133 Undecorated rim sherd. Light brown to greyish brown both faces. A row of perforations made before firing set beneath the rim. Fabric: 2 M F. Rim diam. 24cm.
-

134 Undecorated rim sherd. Grey to reddish brown both faces. Remains of a row of perforations made before firing set beneath the rim. Fabric: 1 S Sh; 1 G.
4S

135 Undecorated rim sherd. Light brown externally, light brown to grey internally. A perforation made before firing beneath the rim. Fabric: 2 M G.
6

136 2 undecorated rim sherds, joining. Light brown externally, brown to grey internally with dark grey core. A row of widely spaced perforations made before firing set beneath the rim. Fabric: 2 L Sh; 1 M G. Rim diam. 26cm.
5F3

137 Undecorated rim sherd. Light brown to grey externally, light brown internally. A row of perforations made before firing set beneath the rim. Fabric: 2 M F. Rim diam. 30 cm.
-

138 4 rim sherds. Light brown externally, light brown to grey internally, with dark grey core. Decoration: On the rim, diagonal slashes. A row of perforations made before firing set beneath the rim. Fabric: 1 S Sh; 2 L G. Rim diam. 22cm.
5F2

139 Undecorated rim sherd. Brown both faces with dark grey core. A perforation made before firing beneath the rim. Fabric: 1 M Sh; 1G.
-

140 Undecorated rim sherd. Light brown externally, grey internally. A perforation made before firing beneath the rim. Fabric: 1 L F; 2 M G.
-

141 Undecorated rim sherd. Grey externally, brown internally. A row of perforations made before firing set beneath the rim. Fabric: 2 M F.
-

142 Undecorated rim sherd. Light brown to grey externally, light brown internally with dark grey core. Remains of a perforation made before firing beneath the rim. Fabric: 1 S Sh; 2 G.
4S

143 Undecorated rim sherd. Light brown to grey externally, brown to grey internally. Remains of a perforation made before firing beneath the rim. Fabric: 1 M F.
-

144 Undecorated rim sherd. Grey to brown both faces. A row of perforations made before firing set beneath the rim. Fabric: 2 G.
'Kit. Site'

145 2 rim sherds, base angle and fragment of base. Light grey both faces. Decoration: On the rim, diagonal slashes. Remains of a row of perforations made before firing set beneath the rim. Fabric: 1 S Sh; 1 G.
-

146 Rim sherd. Light brown to grey externally, light brown internally, with grey core. Decoration: On the rim, diagonal slashes. A row of perforations made before firing set beneath the rim. Fabric: 1 S Sh; 1 G. Rim diam. 30cm.

-

147 Rim sherd. Light brown to grey externally, grey internally. Decoration: On the rim, incised herringbone. A row of perforations made before firing set beneath the rim. Fabric: 1 S Sh; 1 G. Rim diam. 24cm.

148 Rim sherd. Light brown both faces. Decoration: On the rim, diagonal slashes with finger tip impressions super-imposed. A perforation made before firing beneath the rim. Fabric: 2 M F.
7F4

149 2 joining rim sherds. Light brown externally, grey internally. Decoration: On the rim, finger tip impressions. Fabric: 2 L G. Rim diam. 10 cm.
5B6

150 2 rim sherds. Light brown to grey both faces. Decoration: On the rim, diagonal slashes. A row of perforations made before firing set beneath the rim. Fabric: 2 G. Rim diam. 18cm.
7

151 Rim sherd. Brownish grey both faces, with dark grey core. Decoration: On the rim, finger tip impressions. Fabric: 2 L G. Rim diam. 16cm.

-

152 Rim sherd. Brown both faces with grey core. Decoration: On the rim, deep finger tip impressions. Fabric: 2 L G. Rim diam. 24cm.
4F3

153 Rim sherd. Brown to grey externally, dark grey internally. Decoration: On the rim, finger tip impressions. Fabric: 2 L G (+ a little chalk).
8C4

154 Rim sherd. Light brown both faces. Decoration: On the rim, finger tip impressions. Fabric: 2 M Sh.

-

155 Rim sherd. Brown to grey both faces with grey core. Decoration: On the rim, finger tip impressions. Fabric: 1 L F; 2 G. Rim diam. 12 cm.

-

156 Rim sherd. Light brown to grey externally, grey internally. Decoration: On the rim, finger tip impressions. Fabric: 2 M G.

-

157 Rim sherd. Light greyish brown externally, grey to brown internally. Decoration: On the rim, finger tip impressions. Fabric: 2 L G. Rim diam. 12cm.

-

158 Rim sherd. Light brown to grey both faces. Decoration: On the rim, a row of fingertip impressions. Fabric: 2 M G. Rim diam. 30 cm.
'Black Hole Kit. Site'.

159 Rim sherd. Light brown both faces with grey core. Decoration: On the rim, a row of fingertip impressions. Fabric: 1 S Sh; 2 S G.

-

160 Rim sherd. Brown both faces. Decoration: On the rim, a row of finger tip impressions. Fabric: 2 M G; 1 M Ch.
3EIA

161 Rim sherd. Light brown both faces with light grey core. Decoration: On the rim, diagonal slashes. Fabric: 1 M F; 2 G.

-

162 Rim sherd. Grey throughout. Decoration: On the rim, diagonal slashes. Remains of two perforations made before firing beneath the rim. Fabric: 1 M Sh.

-

163 Rim sherd. Light brown to grey externally, grey internally. Decoration: On the rim, diagonal slashes. Fabric: 1 S Sh; 2 L G. Rim diam. 32cm.
6E3

164 Rim sherd. Grey externally, light brown internally. Decoration: On the rim, diagonal slashes. Fabric: 2 S Sh. Rim diam: 24 cm.
6S

165 Rim sherd. Greyish brown both faces. Decoration: On the rim, diagonal slashes. Fabric: 1 S G.

-

166 Rim sherd. Light brown to grey externally. Grey internally. Decoration: On the rim, one diagonal slash. Fabric: 1 M Sh; 1 L G.

-

167 Rim sherd. Light brown to grey both faces. Decoration: On the rim, diagonal slashes. Fabric: 1 M Sh.
6C4

168 Rim sherd. Grey throughout. Decoration: On the external edge of the rim, diagonal slashes. Fabric: 3 S Sh.

-

169 Rim sherd. Light brown to grey externally, grey internally. Decoration: On the rim, diagonal slashes. Fabric: 2 M G.
5D6

170 Rim sherd. Light brown both faces with grey core. Decoration: On the rim, diagonal slashes. Fabric: 2 L G. Rim diam. 14 cm.

-

171 Rim sherd. Light brown throughout. Decoration: On the rim, diagonal impression. Fabric: 1 S Sh; 2 M G.

-

172 Rim sherd. Light brown both faces, with light grey core. Decoration: On the rim, diagonal slashes. Fabric: 2 L G.
8F4

173 2 joining rim sherds. Light brown to grey both faces with dark grey core. Decoration: On the rim, diagonal slashes. Fabric: 1 M F, some Ch. Rim diam. 27cm.
G34

174 Rim sherd. Brown externally, grey internally. Decoration: On the rim, diagonal slashes. A diagonal slash on the body beneath the rim. Fabric: 1 M F.

-

175 2 rim sherds. Light brown to grey externally, light brown internally. Decoration: On the rim, diagonal slashes. Fabric: 1 S Sh. Rim diam. 22cm.
4F4

176 Rim sherd. Grey externally, light brown internally. Decoration: On the rim, diagonal slashes. On the body, a row of diagonal finger nail impressions. Fabric: 1 M F; G.
5F5

177 Rim sherd. Light brown to grey both faces. Decoration: On the rim, diagonal slashes. Fabric: 2 M G.

-

178 Rim sherd. Light brown both faces with dark grey core. Decoration: On the rim, diagonal slashes. Fabric: 2 M G. Rim diam. 11 cm.

-

179 Rim sherd. Light brown to grey externally, grey internally. Decoration: On the rim, diagonal slashes. On the body, a row of diagonal slashes. Fabric: 2 M G. Rim diam. 16 cm.

-

180 Rim sherd. Light brown both faces with grey core. Decoration: On the rim, diagonal slashes. Fabric: 1 S Sh; G.

-

181 2 rim sherds. Light brown externally, grey internally. Decoration: On the rim, diagonal slashes. On the body, remains of diagonal slashes. Fabric: 1 M F; G. Rim diam. ?20 cm.

-

182 Rim sherd. Light brown to grey externally, light brown internally. Decoration: On the external edge of the rim, diagonal slashes. Fabric: 2 M G. Rim diam. 10cm.

-

183 Rim sherd. Light brown both faces with grey core. Decoration: On the external edge of the rim, diagonal slashes. Fabric: 1 M Sh; 2 M G.
3

184 Rim sherd. Light brown externally, grey internally. Decoration: On the rim, diagonal slashes. Fabric: 1 M Sh; G.
4F2

185 Rim sherd. Light brown both faces. Decoration: On the rim, diagonal slash. Fabric: 1 M G.
-

186 5 rim sherds, 2 joining. Grey to brown both faces. Decoration: On the rim, diagonal slashes. Fabric: 1 Sh; 1 M F; G.
6, 'Kit. Site'

187 2 rim sherds. Light brown externally, brown to grey internally. Decoration: On the rim, diagonal slashes. Fabric: 1 S Sh; G. Rim diam. 12cm.
-

188 Rim sherd. Light brown externally, brown to grey internally. Decoration: On the rim, diagonal slashes. Fabric: 1 S Sh.
-

189 Rim sherd. Light brown externally, grey internally. Decoration: On the rim, diagonal slashes. Fabric: 2 M G. Rim diam. 20cm.
5B6

190 Rim sherd. Grey to brown externally, brown internally. Decoration: On the rim, diagonal slashes. Fabric: 2 M F; G. Rim diam. 30cm.
-

191 Rim sherd. Grey externally, light brown internally. Decoration: On the rim, diagonal slashes. Fabric: 2 M Sh; G.
7E6

192 Rim sherd. Light brown both faces with grey core. Decoration: On the rim, a diagonal slash. Fabric: 1 S Sh; G.
-

193 Rim sherd. Light brownish grey, internal surface lost. Decoration: On the rim, diagonal slashes or finger nail impressions. Fabric: 1 M Sh; G.
-

194 Rim sherd. Light brown both faces, with grey core. Decoration: On the rim, diagonal slashes. Fabric: 1 M Sh; G.
-

195 3 rim sherds, joining. Light brown to grey externally, grey to brown internally. Decoration: On the rim, diagonal slashes. Fabric: 1 S Sh; G. Rim diam. 13 cm.
7D4

196 2 rim sherds. Grey both faces. Decoration: On the rim, diagonal slashes. Remains of knob. Fabric: 2 M G. Rim diam. 14 cm.
-

196a Rim sherd. External surface lost. Internally light brown. Decoration: On the rim, diagonal slash and indefinite impression. Fabric: 2 M G (not illustrated).
-

197 Rim sherd. Light brown both faces. Decoration: On the rim, diagonal slashes. Fabric: 1 S F; G.
-

198 Rim sherd. Brown both faces with grey core. Decoration: On the rim, incised herringbone. Fabric: 1 S Sh.
-

199 2 rim sherds and one wall sherd. Light brown to grey both faces. Decoration: On the rim, diagonal slashes and indefinite impressions. On the shoulder cordon, diagonal slashes. Fabric: 1 S Sh; G. Rim diam. 18.5 cm.
5E3, 7E3

200 3 rim sherds, 2 joining, and 6 wall sherds. Light brown externally, light brown to grey internally. Decoration: On the rim, diagonal/opposed slashes. On the shoulder cordon, vertical slashes. Fabric: 3 G; very occasional M Sh. Rim diam. 18.6 cm.
4F1A, 4F3

201 Rim and wall sherd. Grey both faces. Decoration: Applied undecorated knobs. Fabric: 1 M Sh; G. Rim diam. 10 cm.
-

202 Rim sherd. Light brown externally, grey internally with grey core. Decoration: Applied undecorated knob. Fabic: 1 M Sh; G; Some Ch. Rim diam. 12 cm.
-

203 Rim sherd. Light brown externally, light brown to grey internally. Decoration: On the shoulder cordon, a diagonal slash. Fabric: 2 S Sh; 1 L Sh.
4F5

204 Rim and 2 wall sherds, joining. Grey to brown externally, grey internally, with dark grey core. Decoration: Applied knobs. Fabric: 2 M G.
F56

205   Rim sherd. Grey to brown both faces. Decoration: Applied knob. Fabric: 1 S Sh; G. Rim diam. 14 cm.
7F3

206   Rim sherd. Light brown both faces. Scar from applied knob. Fabric: 1 S Sh; G.
3G4

207   Rim sherd. Grey externally, grey to brown internally. Decoration: Applied knob. Fabric: 2 M G. Rim diam. 12 cm.
7

208   Rim sherd. Light brown throughout. Decoration: Applied knob. Fabric: 1 S Sh; 1 G. Rim diam. 13 cm.
-

209   Wall sherd. Light brown both faces. Scar from applied knob. Fabric: 1 S Sh; G.
5D4

210   Rim sherd. Light brown externally, light brown to grey internally. Decoration: Applied knobs. Fabric: 1 M Sh; 1 G. Rim diam. 10 cm.
-

211   Rim sherd. Light brown to grey externally, grey internally. Scar from applied knob. Decoration: On scar and body, short comb lines. Fabric: 1 G.
5E3

212   3 wall sherds. Light brown externally, grey internally. Decoration: Applied knobs. Fabric: 1 S Sh; 2 G.
4S

213   Wall sherd. Light brown both faces. Decoration: Applied knob. Fabric: 2 M G.
6

214   Wall sherd. Grey to brown externally, grey internally . Decoration: Applied knob. Fabric: 1 S Sh; G.
8C3

215   Wall sherd. Light brown both faces with grey core. Decoration: Applied knob. Fabric: 1 S F 'Kit. Site'.

216   Wall sherd. Brown both faces with grey core. Decoration: Applied knob. Fabric: 1 S Sh; G.
-

217   Rim sherd. Light brown externally, grey internally. Decoration: On the rim, a deep transverse impression. Fabric: 2 M F; G.
-

218   Rim sherd. Light brown to grey externally, light brown internally with grey core. Decoration: On the rim, a row of ? bone impressions. Fabric: 1 M Sh; G. Rim diam. 28 cm.
-

219   Rim sherd. Light brown to grey both faces. Decoration: On the rim, a transverse impression. Beneath the rim, a pair of impressions. Fabric: G.
-

220   Rim sherd: Brown externally, grey internally. Decoration: On the rim a row of impressions. Fabric: 2 M G.
-

221   Rim sherd. Grey externally, dark grey internally. Decoration: On the rim, impressions set in herringbone fashion. Fabric: 2 M G. Rim diam. 14 cm.
-

221a   Rim sherd. Greyish brown both faces. Decoration: On the rim, indefinite impression. Fabric: 1 M Sh; 3 M G (not illustrated).
-

222   2 wall sherds. Light brown both faces. Decoration: On the shoulder cordon, incised herringbone. Fabric: 2 M G; Some Ch.
5E4

223   Wall sherd. Light brown both faces. Decoration: On the shoulder cordon, incised herringbone. Fabric: 2 M G.
5B5

224   4 wall sherds, 3 joining. Light brown to grey both faces with grey core. Decoration: On the shoulder cordon, incised herringbone. Fabric: 2 S Sh; 1 M Sh; G.
4F5

225   2 joining wall sherds. Light brown externally, grey internally. Decoration: On the shoulder cordon, incised herringbone. Fabric: 2 M G.
5F1

226 Wall sherd. Light brown to grey externally, grey internally. Decoration: On the shoulder cordon, incised herringbone. Fabric: 1 M F; G.
3S

227 Wall sherd. Light brown to grey externally, light brown internally with grey core. Decoration: On the shoulder cordon, incised herringbone. Fabric: 1 M F; G.
4

228 Wall sherd. Grey externally, light brown to grey internally. Decoration: On the shoulder cordon, incised herringbone. Fabric: 1 M F; G.
6F2

229 Wall sherd. Greyish brown externally, brown internally. Decoration: On the shoulder cordon, impressed herringbone. Fabric: 1 S Sh; G.
-

230 2 rim sherds. Light brown both faces with grey core. Decoration: On the outer edge of the rim, diagonal incised lines. Fabric: G; very sparse Ch.
5

231 Wall sherd. Light brown to grey externally, grey internally. Decoration: Incised herringbone. Fabric: 1 M G.
-

232 Wall sherd. Light brown both faces with grey core. Decoration: Remains of incised herringbone. Fabric: 2 G.
4

233 Wall sherd. Light brown to grey both faces. Decoration: On the shoulder cordon, incised herringbone. Fabric: 1 M F; G.
-

234 Rim and 3 wall sherds. Light brown to grey both faces. Decoration: On the rim, diagonal slashes. On the body, irregularly placed finger nail impressions. Fabric: 1 M F; 2G.
-

235 2 undecorated joining rim sherds. Grey both faces. Drill-hole in wall made before firing. Fabric: 2 S F; G. Rim diam. 28 cm.
7

236 Rim and 3 wall sherds, joining. Brown both faces with dark grey core. Decoration: On the shoulder cordon, a row of diagonal finger tip impressions. Fabric: 3 M F. Rim diam. 16 cm.
4

237 Wall sherd. Light brown throughout. Decoration: A row of finger nail impressions. Fabric: 2 M G.
-

237a 2 wall sherds. Light greyish brown externally, grey internally. Decoration: Irregular finger nail impressions. Fabric: 1 M F; G (not illustrated).
-

238 3 wall and 1 base angle sherd. Light brown to grey both faces. Decoration: On the body, irregular finger nail impressions. Fabric: 2 M F; G; occasional Sh.
4F2, 7F4.

238a Wall sherd. Brown both faces with dark grey core. Decoration: Light finger nail impressions. Fabric: 1 M F; G (not illustrated).
-

239 8 sherds from vessel, 2 pairs joining. Greyish brown externally, grey internally. Decoration: On the rim, transverse finger tip impressions. On the body, horizontal/diagonal row of finger nail impressions. Fabric: 2 M G. Rim diam: 10.5 cm.
5E2

240 2 joining rim sherds. Light brown to grey externally, brown internally with grey core. Decoration: On the shoulder cordon, a row of diagonal finger tip impressions. Fabric: 1 M F; G. Rim diam. 18 cm.
4F1A, 7D4

241 Rim sherd. Grey externally, brown internally. Decoration: On the shoulder cordon, a row of diagonal finger nail/tip impressions. Fabric: 1 S F; G. Rim diam. 13 cm.
5F3

242 Rim sherd. Greyish brown externally, grey internally. Decoration: On the shoulder cordon, diagonal finger tip impressions. Fabric: 2 M G.
-

243   Wall sherd. Light brown both faces with dark grey core. Decoration: On the shoulder cordon, a row of diagonal finger tip impressions. Fabric: 1 M Sh.

-

244   Wall sherd. Brown both faces. Decoration: On the ? shoulder, finger nail/tip impressions. Fabric: 1 S Sh; 3 G.

-

245   Wall sherd. Light brown both faces with dark grey core. Decoration: On the shoulder cordon a row of elongated thumb impressions. Fabric: 1 S Sh, 1 M F.
5B6

245a   Wall sherd. Light brown externally, internal surface lost. Decoration: On the shoulder cordon, remains of elongated thumb impressions. Fabric: 1 S Sh. (not illustrated).

-

246   Wall sherd. Light brown both faces. Decoration: On the shoulder cordon, diagonal finger tip impressions. Fabric: 3 G; occasional Sh.
4-5

247   15 sherds from a vessel including rim, base angle and base. Light brown both faces, with dark grey core. Decoration: On top of the rim, remains of short diagonal point toothed comb lines. On the external edge of the rim, diagonal incised lines above finger tip impressions with irregular point toothed comb lines above and on the body down to the base. Further point toothed comb lines internally on the wall and base. Fabric: 2 L G.

-

248   Wall sherd. Light brown to grey externally, light brown internally with grey core. Decoration: On the shoulder cordon, diagonal slashes. Fabric: 1 M Sh; 2 G.

-

249   Wall sherd. Greyish brown externally, grey internally. Decoration: On the shoulder cordon, diagonal slashes. Fabric: 1 M F; G.
5E2

250   Wall sherd. Light brown to grey externally, grey internally. Decoration: On the shoulder cordon, diagonal slashes. Fabric: 1 M F.
7D4

251   2 wall sherds. Light brown externally, greyish brown internally. Decoration: On the shoulder cordon, diagonal slashes. Fabric: 2 M Sh; 1 G.
4S

252   20 sherds, 15 joining, including approximately half of the rim of a vessel. Light brown to grey both faces with dark grey core. Decoration: On the rim, and on the shoulder cordon, diagonal slashes. Fabric: 2 M F; G. Rim diam. 24 cm.
4F2, 4F4, 5E3, 5E4, 5E6, 7D3, 7E3, 7E4, 8E4.

253   Wall sherd. Brown externally, brown to grey internally. Decoration: Beneath the rim, a row of perforations made before firing. On the shoulder cordon, diagonal slashes. Fabric: 1 S Sh; G.
6G4

254   Wall sherd. Light brown both faces. Decoration: On the shoulder cordon, diagonal slashes. Fabric: 2 L Sh; 2 G.
4.

255   Wall sherd. Light brown to grey externally. Light grey internally with grey core. Decoration: On the shoulder cordon, remains of diagonal slashes. Fabric 1 S Sh; G.

-

256   Wall sherd. Light brown to grey externally, light brown to dark grey internally. Decoration: On the shoulder cordon, diagonal slashes. Fabric: 1 S Sh; G.

-

257   Wall sherd. Light brown both faces. Decoration: On the shoulder cordon, diagonal slashes. Fabric: 1 M F; G; some Ch.

-

258   3 rim sherds with 1 wall. Light brown to grey both faces. Decoration: On the external surface horizontal to diagonal striations. Fabric: 2 L G; occasional F and Sh.
7D4

259 2 wall sherds. Light brown to grey externally, grey internally. Decoration: On the shoulder cordon, a row of deep finger tip impressions. On the wall above, horizontal/ diagonal striations. Fabric: 1 M F; G.
-

260 Wall sherd. Light greyish brown both faces with dark grey core. Decoration: On the shoulder, a faint vertical impression. Fabric: 1 M Sh.
-

261 Undecorated wall. Grey both faces. Fabric: G.
-

262 Base. Light brown to grey internally, external surface lost. Decoration: Finger tip impressions. Fabric: G.
-

263 Base. Greyish brown internally, light brown externally. Decoration: Finger tip impressions. Fabric: G.
5F3

264 Base angle. Light greyish brown externally, grey internally. Fabric: 1 S Sh; G.
5

265 2 joining base angle sherds. Light brown externally, grey internally. Fabric: 2 G.
F55

266 2 joining base angles. Light brown externally, light brown to grey internally. Fabric: 1 M Sh; G.
4E2, 4F2

267 2 joining base angle sherds. Light brown externally, grey internally. Fabric: G.
-

268 Base angle. Light brown externally, grey internally. Fabric: 1 S Sh; G.
-

269 3 base angle sherds, 2 joining. Light brown externally, grey internally. Fabric: 1 M F; G.
8D4, 5E2

270 Base angle: Brown externally, grey internally. Fabric: 1 S Sh; G.
-

271 Base angle. Brown both faces. Fabric: 2 S F.
-

272 Base angle. Light brown externally, grey internally. Fabric: 2 L Sh; G.
-

273 2 joining base angles. Light brown externally, grey intenally. Fabric: 1 S Sh.
-

274 Base angle. Light brown externally, internal surface lost. Fabric: 1 S Sh; G.
6F3

275 2 joining base angle sherds. Light greyish brown both faces with dark grey core. Fabric: 2 M F; G.
6E9, 7D4

276 2 joining base angle sherds, light brown to light greyish brown externally, grey internally. Fabric: 2 M F; 1 S Sh.
5E2, 7E3

277 7 joining sherds of base angle. Light brown externally, grey internally. Fabric: 1 S Sh; G.
5C4

278 7 joining sherds of base angle. Light brown to grey both faces. Fabric: 1 M Sh; some F.
-

OPPENHEIMER COLLECTION: SECTION 7

279 Plain rim sherd. Brown to grey externally, light brown to grey internally. Fabric: 1 M Sh; G. Rim diam: 30 cm.
1917, 11-5, 69

280 Plain rim sherd. Light brown both faces. A row of perforations made before firing beneath the rim. Fabric: 1 M Sh; G.
1917, 11-5, 70

281 Plain rim sherd. Grey both faces. Pit made before before firing beneath the rim. Fabric: 1 M F; 1 L F.

282 2 rim sherds. Grey to brown externally, reddish brown to grey internally. Decoration: On the rim, diagonal incised lines. A row of perforations made before firing beneath the rim. An applied knob on the body. Fabric: 1 S F; G. Rim diam: 18 cm.
1917, 11-5, 61 & 62

283 Rim sherd. Grey to brown both faces. Decoration: On the rim, diagonal incised lines. A row of perforations made before firing beneath the rim. Fabric: 2 M Sh; G. Rim diam: 16 cm.
1917, 11-5, 65

284 Fragment of base or lid. Brown both faces. Perforation through the wall made before firing. Fabric: 1 M Sh.

285 Rim and joining wall sherd. Brown to reddish brown and grey externally, grey internally. Decoration: On the rim, diagonal incised lines. Fabric: 1 S Sh.
1917, 11-5, 66

286 Rim sherd. Light brown to grey externally, grey internally. Decoration: On the rim, diagonal strokes. Fabric: G.
1917, 11-5, 68

287 Rim and, 3 joining wall sherds. Light brown to greyish brown externally, light brown internally. Decoration: On the shoulder cordon, finger tip impressions. Fabric: 1 S F; 1Sh. Smith (1915) 212, fig. 82.
1917, 11-5,72

288 2 joining rim sherds. Light brown externally, light brown to grey internally. Decoration: On the outside edge of the rim, diagonal strokes. Fabric: G. Rim diam. 12 cm.
1917 11-5, 64

289 Rim sherd. Light brown to greyish brown externally, grey internally. Decoration: On the rim, transverse strokes. Fabric: 1 S F; G.
1917, 11-5, 67

290 Rim sherd. Light brown both faces. Decoration: On the rim, diagonally applied opposed finger tip impressions. Fabric: 1 M Sh. Rim diam. 14 cm.
1917, 11-5, 63

291 2 joining rim sherds. Light brown both faces. Applied knob on the body. Fabric: G; occasional Sh.
1917, 11-5, 73.

292 Wall sherd. Light brown to grey externally, internal surface lost. Decoration: On the shoulder cordon, diagonal incised lines. Fabric: 1 S Sh; G.
1917, 11-5, 56A

293 Wall sherd. Grey externally, dark grey internally. Undecorated shoulder cordon. Fabric: 1 M F; G.
1917, 11-5, 57

294 Wall sherd. Light brown to grey externally, grey to dark grey internally. Undecorated shoulder cordon. Fabric: 1 M Sh; G.
1917, 11-5, 59

295 Wall sherd. Grey both faces. Undecorated shoulder cordon. Fabric: 1 M F.
1917, 11-5, 58

296 Undecorated rim sherd. Light brown to grey externally, dark grey internally. Fabric: 1 S Sh; G.
1917, 11-5, 92

297 Plain rim and joining wall sherd. Light brown to grey externally, grey internally. Fabric: 1 M Sh; G.
1917, 11-5, 71

298 2 fragments of base angle. Light brown to grey externally, grey internally. Decoration: On the body, diagonal incised lines. 1 L Sh.
1917, 11-5, 77

299 Rim sherd. Light brown to grey both faces. Decoration: On the rim, irregularly placed transverse and diagonal strokes. Fabric: 1 S Sh; G. Rim diam: 16cm.

300 Base angle. Light brown externally, grey internally. Fabric: 1 S F.

301 2 joining base angles. Brown to grey externally, grey internally. Fabric: 1 S Sh; G.
1917, 11-5, 78 & 79

302 Base angle. Light brown externally, brown internally. Fabric: 1 M Sh; G.
1917, 11-5, 75

303   2 joining base angles. Light brown externally, light brown to grey internally. Fabric: 1 S Sh; G.
1917, 11-5, 74

BRITISH MUSEUM EXCAVATIONS

304   2 undecorated rim sherds, joining. Brown to grey externally, light brown internally. Fabric 1 S Sh; 2 G. Rim diam. 32 cm.
75: L1462 1275.5/905.5 5 G

305   2 undecorated rim sherds. Light brown externally, grey internally. Fabric: 2 M Sh. Rim diam. 19 cm.
76: L1772, L2202 1270/900 18H, 20 I

306   Undecorated rim sherd. Light brown externally, light brown to grey internally. Fabric: 2 G. Rim diam. 33cm.
75: L1182 1275.5/905.5 4 I

307   Undecorated rim sherd. Light brown externally, light brown to dark grey internally. Fabric: 1 M Sh; G. Rim diam. 18 cm.
75: L1039 1270.5/905.5 Topsoil

308   3 undecorated rim sherds joining. Grey both faces. Fabric: 1 M F.
76: L2507 1270/900 19c D

309   Undecorated rim sherd. Brown externally, grey to brown internally, grey core. Fabric: Nil.
76: L2338 1275.5/905.5 12

310   2 undecorated rim sherds and 2 wall, 3 joining. Greyish brown externally, grey internally. Fabric: 1 S F; G. Rim diam. 16 cm.
75: L1366 & L1367 1325.5/970.5 Feature 2 7

311   4 undecorated rim sherds, 2 joining. Grey to light brown both faces. Fabric: G. Rim diam. 13cm.
75: L1451, L1452; 76: L1857 & 1878 1270/900 14B, 17 B, 19c C, 20a C

312   Undecorated rim sherd. Brown externally, brown to grey internally. Fabric: G.
75: L1119 1270.5/905.5 3

313   Undecorated rim sherd. Grey externally, brown internally. Fabric: G.
75: L1081 1275.5/905.5 2

314   Undecorated rim sherd. Grey externally, light brown internally. Fabric: G.
76: L1585 1275.5/905.5 6 N

315   Undecorated rim sherd. Grey externally, brown internally. Fabric: G.
75: L1131 1270/900 13 G

316   Undecorated rim sherd. Greyish brown both faces. Fabric: 1 S F.
75: L1469 1325.5/970.5 Feature 2 7

317   Undecorated rim sherd. Grey both faces. Fabric: 1 S F; G.
76: L2175 1275.5/900.5 4

318   Undecorated rim sherd. Light brown to grey externally, grey internally. Fabric: 1 S Sh.
76: L1664 1270/900 13 I

319   Undecorated rim sherd. Brown externally, grey internally. Fabric: G.
75: L1180 1275.5/905.5 4 F

320   Undecorated rim sherd. Brown to grey externally, grey internally. Fabric: G; some F.
75: L1329 1270/900 14 G

321   Undecorated rim sherd. Brown both faces. Fabric: G.
75: L1081 1275.5/905.5 2

322   Undecorated rim sherd. Brown externally, grey internally. Fabric: 1 S Sh.
74: L226 1270.5/900.5 3

323   Undecorated rim sherd. Light brown externally, light brown to grey internally. Fabric: G.
76: L1575 1275.5/905.5 6 K

324   Undecorated rim sherd. Brown both faces. Fabric: 1 M Sh; G.
74: L556 1270.5/900.5 2

325   Undecorated rim sherd. Light brown externally, grey internally. Fabric: 1 S F.
76: L1648 1270/900 18 C

326   Undecorated rim sherd. Light brown both faces. Fabric: G.
75: L1185 1275.5/905.5 4 J

327   Undecorated rim sherd. Grey both faces. Fabric: G.
76: L1925 1275.5/900.5 4B-D, F-H

328   Undecorated rim sherd. Grey externally, brown to grey internally. Fabric: 1 M F.
76: L2451 1270/900 20/21

329   Undecorated rim sherd. Greyish brown both faces. Fabric: G.
76: L1570 1275.5/905.5 6 J

330   Undecorated rim sherd. Brown to grey both faces. Fabric: G.
75: L1443 1275.5/900.5 5 I

331   Undecorated rim sherd. Greyish brown externally, grey internally. Fabric: Some S.
76: L2345 1270/900 20a D

332   Undecorated rim sherd. Grey both faces. Fabric: 1 M Sh.
76: L2334 1270/900 20a D

333   Undecorated rim sherd. Grey externally, light grey internally. Fabric: 2 L Sh.
76: L1772 1270/900 18 H

334   Undecorated rim sherd. Grey both faces. Fabric: 1 M Sh.
76: L2345 1270/900 20a D

335   Undecorated rim sherd. Light brown both faces. Fabric: G.
75: L1405 1275.5/905.5 5 F

336   Undecorated rim sherd. Greyish brown both faces. Fabric: 1 M Sh.
76: L1895 1270/900 20a C

337   Undecorated rim sherd. Light brown to grey externally, light brown internally. Fabric: 1 S Sh.
76: L1939 1275.5/905.5 6 K

338   Undecorated rim sherd. Brown both faces. Fabric: 1 S Sh; G.
76: L1766 1270/900 18 0

339   Undecorated rim sherd. Brown both faces. Fabric: G.
76: L1575 1275.5/905.5 6K

340   3 undecorated rim sherds, joining. Light brown to grey both faces. Fabric: 1 S Sh; G. Rim diam. 22 cm.
76: L1570 & L1714 1275.5/905.5 6 J & M

341   Undecorated rim sherd. Light brown to grey externally, grey internally. Fabric: 1 S Sh; G.
76: L1779 l270/900 18 M

342   Undecorated rim sherd. Light greyish brown both faces. Fabric: 1 S Sh; some S.
76: L2144 1270/900 20a D

343 Undecorated rim sherd. Brown both faces. Fabric: 1 S F; G.
72: M234 1270.5/901.1 Feature 1

344   Undecorated rim sherd. Grey both faces. Fabric: 1 M F.
75: L1386 1275.5/905.5 5 E

345   Undecorated rim sherd. Brown both faces. Fabric: 1 S Sh.
72: M212 1255.5/911.1 Chalk 5 O

346   Undecorated rim sherd. Brown externally, grey internally. Fabric: 1 S Sh; G.
75: L1386 1275.5/905.5 5 E

347   Undecorated rim sherd. Light brown to grey externally, grey internally. Fabric: 1 S Sh.
76: L1645 1270/900 13 C

348   Undecorated rim sherd. Light brown to grey externally, light brown internally. Fabric: 1 S Sh.
76: L1885 1270/900 20 D

349   Undecorated rim sherd. Light brown externally, grey internally. Fabric: 1 L F.
76: L2451 1270/900 20/21

350   2 undecorated rim sherds, joining. Grey to brown both faces. Fabric: G; some S.
76: L1895 1270/900 20a C

351   Undecorated rim sherd. Grey both faces. Fabric: 1 M Sh; G.
76: L1772 1270/900 18 H

352   Undecorated rim sherd. Light brown both faces. Fabric: 1 S Sh; G.
76:L1725 β42 6

353   Undecorated rim sherd. Grey both faces. Fabric: 1 S Sh; G.
75: L1169 1275.5/905.5 4 O

354   Undecorated rim sherd. Light brown both faces. Fabric G.
75: L1273 1270/900 l5 S

355 Undecorated rim sherd. Grey both faces. Fabric: G.
75: L1467 1270/900 14 L

356 Undecorated rim sherd. Light brown to grey both faces. Fabric: G.
75: L1185 1275.5/905.5 4 J

357 Undecorated rim sherd. Grey both faces. Fabric: S.
76: L1853 β44 6

358 Undecorated rim sherd. Light brown both faces. Fabric: G.
76: L1924 1275.5/900.5 4

359 Undecorated rim sherd. Light brown both faces. Fabric: 1 M F.
76: L2451 1270/900 20/21

360 Rim sherd. Light brown both faces. Decoration: 2 deep finger tip impressions beneath the rim. Fabric: 1 M F.
76: L2451 1270/900 20/21

361 Undecorated rim sherd. Greyish brown externally, light brown internally. Fabric: 1 S Sh; G.
75: L1371 1275.5/905.5 5 F

362 Undecorated rim sherd. Brown both faces. Fabric: G.
75: L1385 1270/900 13 S

363 Undecorated rim sherd. Grey to brown externally, grey internally. Fabric: 1 M F.
76: L2507 1270/900 19c D

364 Undecorated rim sherd. Light brown both faces. Fabric: 1 S F; 1 S Sh.
76: L2328 1275.5/905.5 12

365 Undecorated rim sherd. Grey externally, light brown internally. Fabric: 1 S Sh.
76: L2409 1270/900 20a D

366 Undecorated rim sherd. Grey externally, brown internally. Fabric: 1 S Sh.
75: L1372 1275.5/905.5 5 L

367 Undecorated rim sherd. Grey externally, light brown to grey internally. Fabric: 1 S F.
76: L2150 1270/900 19c C

368 Undecorated rim sherd. Grey externally, brown internally. Fabric: 2 M F.
76: L2569 1270/900 19c E

369 Undecorated rim sherd. Greyish brown both faces. Fabric: G.
75: L1381 1270.5/905.5 4 & 9 M/N cleaning

370 Undecorated rim sherd. Light brown both faces. Fabric: 1 M Sh; G.
76: L1827 1275.5/905.5 6 E

371 Undecorated rim sherd. Grey both faces. Fabric: 1 S Sh; G.
75: L1464 1270/900 16C

372 Rim and 2 wall sherds, joining. Greyish brown externally, grey internally. Decoration: On the rim and on the shoulder cordon, finger tip impressions. Fabric: 1 S Sh; G. Rim diam: 23cm.
75: L1468 1275.5/905.5 5 K

373 Wall sherd. Greyish brown externally, brown internally. Decoration: On the cordon, a row of finger tip impressions. Fabric: 1 M F; G.
76: L2202 1270/900 20 I

374 2 joining wall sherds. Grey externally, brown internally. Decoration: On the cordon, a row of finger tip impressions. Fabric: 1 M F; G.
76: L1721 & L1772 1270/900 18 I, 18 H

375 Wall sherd. Greyish brown both faces. Decoration: On the cordon, a row of finger tip impressions. Fabric: 1 M Sh.
76: L 1578 1275.5/905.5 6 M

376 Wall sherd. Brown externally, brown to grey internally. Decoration: On the cordon, a row of finger tip impressions. Fabric: G; some S.
76: L1564 1275.5/905.5 6 I

377 2 joining wall sherds. Brown both faces. Decoration: On the cordon, a row of finger tip impressions. Fabric: 1 S Sh; G.
75: L1404 & L1461 1275.5/905.5 5E

378 Wall sherd. Brown externally, grey internally. On the cordon, a row of finger tip impressions. Fabric: G; some S.
76: L1539 β42 6

379 Wall sherd. Brown externally, greyish brown internally. Decoration: On the cordon, remains of a row of finger tip impressions. Fabric: G.
75: L1185 1275.5/905.5 4 J

380 Wall sherd. Light brown externally, grey internally. Decoration: On the cordon, a row of finger tip impressions. Fabric: 1 M F.
76: L2262 1270/900 20a I

381 Wall sherd. Light brown both faces. Decoration: On the cordon, remains of a row of finger tip impressions. Fabric: 1 S Sh; G.
75: L1403 1275.5/905.5 10 L Feature 6

382 Wall sherd. Light brown externally, grey internally. Decoration: On the cordon, a row of finger tip impressions. Fabric: 1 S Sh; G.
76: L1570 1275.5/905.5 6 J

383 Wall sherd. Brown both faces. Decoration: On the cordon, a finger tip impression. Fabric: G.
75: L1081 1275.5/905.5 2

384 Wall sherd. Light brown both faces. Decoration: On the cordon, remains of a row of finger tip impressions. Fabric: G.
76: L1620 β43 6

385 Wall sherd. Light brown both faces. Decoration: On the cordon, a row of finger tip impressions. Fabric: 1 M F; G.
75: L1141 1270/900 13 Q

386 Wall sherd. Light brown externally, grey internally. Decoration: On the cordon, a row of finger tip impressions. Fabric: 1 S Sh; G.
75: L1421 1275.5/905.5 5 A

387 Wall sherd. Light brown externally, grey to light brown internally. Decoration: On the cordon, remains of a row of finger tip impressions. Fabric: 1 S Sh; G.
76: L1575 1275.5/905.5 6 K

388 Fragment of cordon. Light brown externally, internal surface lost. Decoration: Indefinitive impression. Fabric: 1 M Sh; G.
75: L1385 1270/900 13 S

389 4 wall sherds. Light brown externally, light brown to dark grey internally. Decoration: On the cordon, deep finger tip impressions. Fabric: 2 L Sh.
76: L1900 1270/900 20 N

390 Wall sherd. Grey both faces. Decoration: On the slight cordon, a row of finger tip impressions. Fabric: 1 L Sh.
76: L2409 1270/900 20a D

391 Wall sherd. Grey externally, greyish brown internally. Decoration: Remains of a finger tip impression. Fabric: 1 M Sh.
76: L2351 1270/900 19a C

392 Wall sherd. Light brown both faces. Decoration: Finger tip impressions. Fabric: 1 L Sh; G.
76: L1891 1270/900 20a I

393 Wall sherd. Brown externally, internal surface lost. Decoration: On the cordon, a row of finger tip impressions. Fabric: 2 S F.
76: L2643 1275.5/900.5 4

394 Wall sherd. Grey both faces. Decoration: A row of diagonally set finger tip impressions. Fabric: 1 L Sh.
75: L1467 1270/900 14 L

395 Wall sherd. Light greyish brown both faces. Decoration: Finger tip impressions. Fabric: 1 L Sh.
76: L2354 1270/900 20a I

396 2 rims and one wall sherd, joining. Brown to grey both faces. A row of closely set perforations made before firing below the rim. Fabric: 1 M Sh; G. Rim diam: 16cm.
76: L1627 & L1925 1275.5/900.5 4 B-D, F-H

397 2 joining rim sherds. Dark grey externally, greyish brown internally. Remains of a row of perforations made before firing below the rim. Fabric: G. Rim diam: 24cm.
75: L1460 & 76: L1656 1270/900 13D, 16C

398 Rim sherd. Brown to grey externally, brown internally. Remains of a row of perforations made before firing below the rim. Fabric: G.
76: L1544 1275.5/905.5 6A

399 Rim sherd. Light brown to grey externally, light brown internally. Remains of a row of perforations made before firing below the rim. Fabric: G. Rim diam: 25.5cm.
76: L2058 1275.5/905.5 6a E

400 Rim sherd. Light brown both faces. Remains of perforations made before firing, below the rim. Fabric: 1 G.
76: L2194 1270.5/905.5 4 0

401 Rim sherd, grey to brown externally, dark grey to brown internally. A row of perforations made before firing below the rim. Fabric: 1 S Sh; G.
75: L1463 1270.5/905.5 4 J

402 Rim sherd. Greyish brown externally, grey to dark grey internally. Perforations made before firing below the rim. Fabric: G.
75: L1445 1270.5/905.5 3 0

403 Rim sherd, grey both faces. Perforations made before firing below the rim. Fabric: 1 M F; G.
76: L1885 1270/900 20 D

404 Rim sherd. Light brown both faces. Decoration: On the rim, a row of finger tip impressions. Remains of a perforation made before firing beneath the rim. Fabric: 1 M/L F.
76: L1823 1270.5/905.5 4 P

405 Rim sherd. Grey both faces. Decoration: On the rim, diagonal slashes. A row of perforations made before firing below the rim. Fabric: Nil.
76: L1827 1275.5/905.5 6 E

406 Rim sherd. Light brown both faces. Decoration: On the rim, diagonal slashes. A perforation made before firing below the rim. Fabric: G.
75: L1463 1270.5/905.5 4 J

407 4 rim sherds, 2 joining. Light brown to grey externally, brown internally. Decoration: On the rim, finger tip impression. A row of perforations made before firing below the rim. Fabric: 1 M F; G. Rim diam. 24cm.
75: L1081, L1185 & L 1324 1275.5/905.5 2, 1275.5/905.5 4 J, 1275.5/900.5 5 E

408 Rim sherd. Dark grey externally, grey internally. Decoration: On the rim, finger tip impressions. A row of perforations made before firing below the rim. Fabric: 3 G. Rim diam. 28cm.
76: L1721 1270/900 18 I

409 Rim and 2 wall sherds, joining. Brown to grey both faces with grey core. Decoration: On the internal and external edges of the rim, diagonally set finger tip impressions. A row of perforations made before firing below the rim. Fabric: 3 M F.
76: L2327 1270/900 22

410 3 rim sherds. Grey to brown both faces. Decoration: On the internal and external edges of the rim, diagonally set finger tip impressions. A row of widely spaced perforations made before firing below the rim. Fabric: 1 M F. Rim diam. 24cm.
76: L2569 & L2649 1270/900 19c E, 22

411 Rim sherd. Light greyish brown externally, light brown internally. Decoration: On the rim, diagonal slashes. A row of perforations made before firing below the rim. Fabric: 1 L F, 1 L Ch.
75: L1406 1270.5/905.5 4N

412 2 rim sherds. Grey to brown both faces. Decoration: On the rim, finger tip impressions. Fabric: 1 M Sh; G.
75: L1233 & L1342 1275.5/905.5 B,G

413 2 rim sherds. Grey both faces. Decoration: On the rim, finger tip impressions. Fabric: 1 S F; G.
75: L1197 & L1460 1270/900 13I, 16C

414 Rim sherd. Light brown both faces. Decoration: On the rim, diagonal finger tip impressions. Fabric: G.
75: L1430 1270.5/905.5 4D

415 Rim sherd. Light brown both faces. Decoration: On the rim, finger tip impressions. Fabric: G.
76: L1564 1275.5/905.5 6 I

416 Rim and wall sherds joining. Greyish brown externally, grey internally. Decoration: On the rim, finger tip impressions. Fabric: 1 L F. Rim diam. 20cm.
75: L1406 1270.5/905.5 4 N

417 Rim sherd. Grey externally, light brown to grey internally. Decoration: On the rim, finger tip impression. Fabric: G.
75: L1468 1275.5/905. 5 5 K

418 Rim sherd. Grey to brown both faces. Decoration: On the rim, finger tip impressions. Fabric: 1 M Sh; G.
75: L1405 1275.5/905.5 5 F

419 2 rim sherds. Brown to grey externally, grey internally. Decoration: On the rim, finger tip impressions. Fabric: G and ?bone. Rim diam. 15cm.
75: L1201 & L1270 1270/900 13M, 15N

420   Rim sherd. Grey both faces. Decoration: On the rim, finger tip impressions. Fabric: 1 S Sh; G. Rim diam. 15cm.
76: L1570 1275.5/905.5 6 J

421   Rim sherd. Grey both faces. Decoration: On the rim, finger tip impressions. Fabric: G; some S.
75: L1150 1275.5/905.5 4 B

422   Rim sherd. Grey to brown externally, light brown internally. Decoration: On the rim, finger tip impressions. Fabric: 1 S F.
76: L1853 β44 6

423   Rim sherd. Grey to brown both faces. Decoration: On the rim, finger tip impressions. Fabric: 1 S S; G.
76: L1620 β43 6

424   Rim sherd. Brown both faces. Decoration: On the rim, finger tip impressions. Fabric: 1 S Sh; G.
75: L1147 1275.5/905.5 4 A

425   Rim sherd. Grey both faces. Decoration: On the rim, finger tip impressions. Fabric: G.
76: L1651 1270/900 13E

426   Rim sherd. Light brown both faces. Decoration: On the rim, finger tip impressions. Fabric: G; some F.
75: L1180 1275.5/905.5 4 F

427   Rim sherd. Grey externally, brown internally. Decoration: On the rim, diagonal finger tip impressions. Fabric: 1 S Sh; G.
76: L1627 1275.5/900.5 4

428   Rim sherd. Brown externally, brown to grey internally. Decoration: On the rim, finger tip impressions. Fabric: 1 S Sh; G.
75: L1248 1270.5/905.5 3 K

429   Rim sherd. Grey to light brown externally, greyish brown internally. Decoration: On the rim, transverse impressions. Fabric: 1 L F; G.
76: L2354 1270/900 20a I

430   Rim sherd. Grey to brown both faces. Decoration: On the rim, diagonal finger tip impressions. Fabric: G.
76: L2202 1270/900 20 I

431   Rim sherd. Light brown both faces. Decoration: On the rim, finger tip impressions. Fabric: G.
72: M294 1260.5/911.1 Chalk 5 N

432   Rim sherd. Light grey externally, light brown internally. Decoration: On the rim, finger tip impressions. Fabric: 1 M Sh.
76: L2409 1270/900 20a D

433   3 rim sherds, 2 joining. Light brown both faces. Decoration: On the rim, deep finger tip impressions. Fabric: 1 L Sh. Rim diam. 24cm.
76: L2354 & L2409 1270/900 20a D, I

434   2 joining rim sherds. Light reddish brown to grey both faces. Decoration: On the rim, finger tip impressions. Fabric: 1 M F. Rim diam. 31cm.
76: L2571 1270/900 19c C

435   Rim sherd. Greyish brown externally, grey to light brown internally. Decoration: On the rim, diagonally placed transverse impressions. Fabric: 1 M F.
76: L2409 1270/900 20a D

436   Rim sherd. Brown externally, greyish brown internally. Decoration: On the rim, finger tip impressions. Fabric: 1 S F.
76: L2374 1270/900 21

437   Rim sherd. Grey externally, brown internally. Decoration: On the rim, diagonal incised lines. Fabric: 1 M Sh. Rim diam. 24cm.
76: L2354 1270/900 20a I

438   Rim sherd. Light brown both faces. Decoration: On the rim, diagonal impressed lines. Fabric: 1 S F; G. Rim diam. 28cm.
76: L1656 1270/900 13 D

439   Rim sherd. Brown externally, grey internally. Decoration: On the rim, diagonal incised lines. Fabric: 1 L F; G.
75: L1311 1275.5/900.5 5 A

440   2 joining rim sherds. Light brown externally, light brown to grey internally. Decoration: On the rim, diagonal incised lines. Fabric: 1 S Sh. Rim diam. 12cm.
76: L1715 & L1803 1275.5/905.5 6 N, M

441   Rim sherd. Greyish brown externally, brown internally. Decoration: On the rim, diagonal incised lines. Fabric: G.
76: L1539 β42 6

442 Rim sherd. Greyish brown externally, grey internally. Decoration: On the rim, diagonal incised lines. Fabric: 2 M F.
76: L1857 1270/900 20a C

443 Rim sherd. Light brown both faces. Decoration: On the rim, diagonal incised lines. Fabric: 1 M F.
76: L1772 1270/900 18 H

444 2 joining rim sherds. Grey both faces. Decoration: On the rim, diagonal incised lines. Fabric: Some S. Rim diam. 22cm.
75: L1462 1275.5/905.5 5 G

445 Rim sherd. Grey externally, grey to brown internally. Decoration: On the rim, diagonal incised lines. Fabric: 1 M Sh; G.
75: L1405 1275.5/905.5 5 F

446 Rim sherd. Grey to light brown externally, light brown internally. Decoration: On the rim, diagonal incised lines. Fabric: 1 S Sh; G.
75: L1270 1270/900 15 N

447 Rim sherd. Light brown both faces. Decoration: On the rim, diagonal incised line. Fabric: 1 L F; G.
76: L1570 1275.5/905.5 6 J

448 Rim sherd. Grey to brown internally. Decoration: On the rim, diagonal incised line. Fabric: 1 M F.
76: L1656 1270/900 13 D

449 Rim sherd. Grey both faces. Decoration: On the rim, diagonal incised lines. Fabric: Nil.
76: L1814 1270/900 19 G

450 Wall sherd. Greyish brown externally, grey internally. Decoration: On the shoulder, a row of finger nail impressions. Fabric: 1 M Sh.
76: L1772 1270/900 18 H

451 Rim sherd. Grey externally, light brown to grey internally. Decoration: On the rim, diagonal incised lines. Fabric: 1 S F; G.
76: L2385 1275.5/900.5 9

451a Rim sherd. Light brown both faces, grey core. Decoration: On top of the rim, diagonal incised lines. Fabric: 1 L F; 2 M Sh.
73: L202 1270.5/900.5 3

452 Rim sherd. Light brown externally, greyish brown internally. Decoration: On the rim, diagonal incised lines. Fabric: 1 M F.
76: L2334 1270/900 20a D

453 3 joining rim sherds. Light brown to grey both faces. Decoration: On the rim, transverse finger tip impressions. Fabric: 1 S F. Rim diam. 17cm.
76: L1823, L1827 & L1853 1270.5/905.5 4 P; 1275.5/905.5 6 E; β44 6

454 Rim sherd. Brown externally, grey internally. Decoration: On the rim, transverse finger tip impressions. Small applied knob beneath the rim. Fabric: 1 S F; G. Diam. 12cm.
75: L1131 1270/900 13 G

455 Rim sherd. Grey to brown externally, grey internally. Decoration: On the rim, diagonal finger tip impressions. Small applied knob beneath the rim. Fabric: 1 S Sh.
75: L1382 1275.5/900.5 14 C

456 Rim sherd. Grey both faces. Small applied knob beneath the rim above ?scar of applied horizontal cordon. Fabric: 1 S Sh. Rim diam. 18cm.
76: L2345 1270/900 20a D

457 Rim sherd. Grey to brown externally, grey internally. Small applied knob beneath the rim. Fabric: G.
76: L1823 1270.5/905.5 4 P

458 Rim sherd, grey to brown externally, lacking internal surface. Remains of 2 small applied knobs beneath the rim. Fabric: 1 S F.
76: L1862 1270/900 20 I

459 Rim sherd. Light brown externally, greyish brown internally. Small applied knob beneath the rim. Fabric: 1 S F.
75: L1190 1270/900 13 D

460 Rim sherd. Grey to brown externally, grey internally. Small applied knob beneath the rim. Fabric: 1 S Sh.
76: L1663 1270/900 18 H

461 Rim sherd. Grey to brown externally, grey internally. Small applied knob beneath the rim. Fabric: G. Rim diam. 13 cm.
76: L1668 1270/900 18 M

462 Wall sherd. Grey externally, brown internally. Applied knob. Fabric: Some S.
76: L2202 1270/900 201

463 Wall sherd. Brown both faces. Applied knob. Fabric: G.
76: L1561 1275.5/905.5 6 H

464 Wall sherd. Light brown externally, grey internally. Applied knob. Fabric: 1 M F.
76: L1838 1270/900 20 N

465 Wall sherd. Brown externally, grey internally. Horizontal perforated lug. Fabric: 1 M F.
75: L1432 1325.5/970.5 7 Feature 2

466 Wall sherd. Light brown externally, grey internally. Applied knob. Fabric: 1 S Sh; G.
76: L1546 1275.5/905.5 6 B

467 Wall sherd. Grey externally, brown internally. Applied knob. Fabric: 1 S Sh.
75: L1197 1270/900 13 I

468 Rim sherd. Greyish brown both faces. Decoration: On the rim, transverse finger tip impressions. Fabric: 1 S Sh. Rim diam: 10cm.
75: L1431 1325.5/970.5 7 Feature 2

469 2 joining rim sherds. Greyish brown externally, brown internally. Decoration: Diagonal impressions. Fabric: 1 S Sh. Rim diam: 11cm.
75: L1266 & L1467 1270/900 14 G, L

470 Wall sherd. Light brown to grey both faces. Applied knob. Fabric: 1 S Sh.
76: L1604 β44 6

471 3 rim sherds, 2 joining. External surface lost, brown internally. Decoration: On the rim, finely incised diagonal lines. Fabric: 1 M F. Rim diam. 12cm. Probably same vessel as 473-4.
75: L1264, 76:L1721 & L1758 1270.5/905.5 3 P; 1270/900 18 I, J

472 2 joining rim sherds. Grey to brown externally, grey internally. Decoration: On the rim, diagonal impressions. On the body, incised rough herringbone crosses. Fabric: 2 S Sh. Rim diam. 18cm.
76: L1570 & L1582 1275.5/905.5 6 J, O

473 Rim sherd. External surface lost. Light brown to grey internally. Decoration: On the rim, finely incised diagonal lines. Fabric: 1 S F. Probably same vessel as 471 and 474.
75: L1192 1270/900 13 H

474 Rim sherd. Light brown to grey both faces. Decoration: On the rim, finely incised circumferential and diagonal lines. Fabric: 1 M F. Probably same vessel as 473.
76: L1597 1270.5/905.5 4 P

475 2 wall sherds. Light brown to grey externally, light brown internally. Decoration: On the cordon, deeply scored diagonal and opposed diagonal lines. Fabric: 2 M/L F.
75: L1459 & L1464 1270.5/905.5 4 O; 1270/900 16 C

476 Wall sherd. Brown both faces. Decoration: Remains of deeply scored herringbone. Fabric: 1 M Sh.
76: L1508 1270.5/905.5/1275.5/905.5 3

477 Rim sherd. Light brown to grey externally, grey internally. Decoration: On the external rim edge, diagonal incised lines. Fabric: 1 S Sh.
75: L1406 1270.5/905.5 4 N

478 Rim sherd. Grey both faces. Decoration: On the external rim edge, diagonal incised lines. Fabric: 2 S Sh; G.
75: L1185 1275.5/905.5 4 J

479 Rim sherd. Greyish brown externally, brown internally. Decoration: On the external rim edge, deeply incised diagonal lines. Fabric: 1 S Sh. Rim diam. 15 cm.
76: L1627 1275.5/900.5 4

480 Rim sherd. Greyish brown externally, brown internally. Decoration: On the external rim edge, remains of deeply incised diagonal lines. Fabric: 1 S Sh; G.
75: L1393 1270.5/905.5 9 N

481 Rim sherd. Grey to greyish brown both faces. Decoration: On the external rim edge, diagonal incised lines. Fabric: G.
76: L1570 1275.5/905.5 6 J

482 Rim sherd. Brown both faces. Decoration: On the external rim edge, vertical incised lines. Fabric: 1 M F.
75: L1398 1325.5/970.5 7 Feature 2

483 Rim sherd. Grey both faces. Decoration: On the external rim edge, diagonal incised lines. Fabric: G.
76: L1575 1275.5/905.5 6 K

484 Rim sherd. Grey both faces. Decoration: On the external rim edge, remains of diagonal incised lines. Fabric: G.
76: L1510 β41 5

485 Rim sherd. Light brown to brown externally, light brown internally. Decoration: On the external rim edge, diagonal incised lines. Fabric: G. Rim diam. 15cm.
75: L1162 1275.5/905.5 4 J

486 Wall sherd. Brown to grey externally, grey internally. Remains of hole drilled after firing. Fabric: 1 M F.
76: L2354 1270/900 20a I

487 Wall sherd. Greyish brown externally, brown internally. Remains of hole drilled after firing. Fabric: Some S.
76: L1721 1270/900 18 I

488 Wall sherd. Greyish brown externally, brown internally. Remains of hole drilled after firing. Fabric: G.
76: L1772 1270/900 18 H

489 Wall sherd. Greyish brown externally, grey internally. Decoration: On the shoulder cordon, finger tip impressions. Fabric: 2 M Sh.
76: L1471 1270/900 18 B/C

490 Wall sherd. Brown both faces. Decoration: On the shoulder cordon, finger tip impressions. Fabric: 1 S F.
75: L1399 1325.5/970.5 7 Feature 2

491 Wall sherd. Light brown externally, internal surface lost. Decoration: On the shoulder cordon, finger tip impressions. Fabric: 1 S Sh.
76: L1575 1275.5/905.5 6 K

492 Wall sherd. Light brown to grey externally, grey internally. Decoration: A row of finger tip impressions. Fabric: G.
75: L1444 1275.5/905.5 5 F

493 Wall sherd. Brown externally, brownish grey internally. Decoration: On the shoulder cordon, finger tip impressions. Fabric: G.
75: L1385 1270/900 13 S

494 Wall sherd. Greyish brown externally, brown internally. Decoration: On the shoulder cordon, finger tip impressions. Fabric: G.
75: L1386 1275.5/905.5 5 E

495 Wall sherd. Grey to light brown externally, grey internally. Decoration: On the shoulder cordon, deep finger tip impressions. Fabric: 2 M F.
76: L2507 1270/900 19c D

496 Wall sherd. Grey externally, dark grey internally. Decoration: On the shoulder cordon, widely spaced finger tip impressions. Fabric: 1 M Sh.
76: L2547 1270/900 19a H

497 Wall sherd. Light brown externally, dark grey internally. Decoration: On the shoulder cordon, deep finger tip impressions. Fabric: 1 L Sh.
76: L2354 1270/900 20a I

498 Wall sherd. Grey both faces. Decoration: On the shoulder cordon, deep finger tip impressions. Fabric: 2 M Sh.
76: L2507 1270/900 19c D

499 Wall sherd. Brown to grey externally, grey internally. Decoration: On the shoulder cordon, remains of widely spaced finger tip impressions. Fabric: 1 S Sh; G.
75: L1203 1270/900 13 0

500 Wall sherd. Light brown both faces. Decoration: On the shoulder cordon, diagonal incised lines. Fabric: 1 S Sh.
75: L1244 1275.5/905.5 4 M

501 Wall sherd. Light brown externally, grey internally. Decoration: On the shoulder cordon, diagonal incised lines. Fabric: 1 S Sh; G.
75: L1185 1275.5/905.5 4 J

502   Wall sherd. Light brown externally, greyish brown internally. Decoration: On the shoulder cordon, diagonal incised lines. Fabric: 2 M Sh.
76: L1663 1270/900 18 H

503   Wall sherd. Brown externally, greyish brown internally. Decoration: On the shoulder cordon, remains of incised herringbone. Fabric: 1 S Sh; G.
75: L1182 1275.5/905.5 4 I

504   Wall sherd. Light brown both faces. Decoration: On the shoulder cordon, a diagonal incised line. Fabric: 2 M F.
76: L1721 1270/900 18 I

505   Wall sherd. Light brown externally, internal surface lost. Decoration: On the shoulder cordon, diagonal incised lines. Fabric: 2 M F.
76: L1721 1270/900 18 I

506   Wall sherd. Grey externally, brown internally. Decoration: Running onto the shoulder cordon, a diagonal incised line. Fabric: G.
76: L1648 1270/900 18 C

507   Wall sherd. Light brown to grey externally, light brown internally. Decoration: Running onto the shoulder cordon, incised diagonal lines. Fabric: 1 L F.
76: L1491 1270/900/1275.5/900.5 5 Feature 9

508   Wall sherd. Light brown externally, brownish grey internally. Decoration: On the shoulder cordon, deep coarse diagonal incised lines. Fabric: G.
76: L2679 1275.5/905.5 6a B

509   3 joining wall sherds. Light brown to grey both faces. Decoration: On the shoulder cordon, diagonal incised lines. Fabric: 1 S Sh; G.
76: L2354 1270/900 20a I

510   Wall sherd. Light brown both faces. Decoration: On the shoulder cordon, diagonal incised lines. Fabric: 1 M Sh.
76: L2451 1270/900 20/21

511   Wall sherd. Light brown externally, grey internally. Decoration: On the shoulder, diagonal incised lines. Fabric 1 M F.
76: L2144 1270/900 20a D

512   4 rim and 3 wall sherds including base angle. Light brown to grey both faces. Decoration: On the rim, shallow finger tip impressions. On the body, short horizontal and diagonal incised strokes. Fabric: G.
75: L1197, L1201 &L1268; 76: L1627 & L2374 1270.5/905.5 6 G; 1270/900 13 I, M; 14 Q; 21; 1275.5/900.5 4

513   Wall sherd, grey externally, brown internally. Decoration: Finely incised lattice. Fabric: Sh.
75: L1259 1275.5/900.5 5 E

514   Wall sherd. Brown externally, grey internally. Plain shoulder cordon. Fabric: 1 S Sh.
75: L1329 1270/900 14 G

515   Wall sherd, greyish brown externally, grey internally. Plain shoulder cordon. Fabric: 1 M Sh.
75: L1392 1270/900 17 L

516   Wall sherd. Greyish brown externally, grey internally. Plain shoulder cordon. Fabric: 1 S F; G.
75: L1329 1270/900 14 G

517   Wall sherd. Light brown externally, light greyish brown internally. Plain shoulder cordon. Fabric: G.
75: L1459 1270.5/905.5 4 O

518   Wall sherd. Light brown externally, grey internally. Plain shoulder cordon. Fabric: 1 M F; G.
75: L1280 1275.5/900.5 5 E

519   Wall sherd. Greyish brown externally, brown to grey internally. Plain curved cordon. Fabric: 1 M Sh.
76: L2409 1270/900 20a D

520   Base angle. Greyish brown externally, grey internally. Fabric: G.
76: L2345 1270.900 20a D

521   Base angle. Light brown externally, grey internally. Fabric: G.
76: L1582 1275.5/905.5 6 O

522   Base angle. Brown both faces. Fabric: 1 S Sh; G.
75: L1446 1270/900 16C

523   Base angle. Brown externally, grey to brown internally. Fabric: G; some Sh; Ch.
75: L1046 1275.5/905.5 Feature 1

524 Base angle. Brown externally, grey internally. Fabric: 1 M F; G.
75: L1440 1270/900 16 M

525 Base angle. Light brown to grey externally, grey internally. Fabric: 1 S Sh; G.
76: L1552 1275.5/905.5 6 E

526 4 joining sherds of wall and base angle. Light brown to grey both faces. Fabric: G.
76: L2631 1270/900 13 C

527 Base angle. Light brown externally, grey internally. Fabric: 1 S Sh; G.
76: L1645 1270/900 13 C

528 5 joining sherds of wall and base angle. Light brown to grey externally, grey internally. Fabric: G.
76: L2409 & L2420 1270/900 20a D & E

529 Base angle and wall sherd, joining. Greyish brown externally, grey internally. Fabric: 1 S Sh; G.
75: L1461 1275.5/905.5 5 E

530 Base angle. Light brown externally, greyish brown internally. Fabric: 1 L F; G. (not illustrated).
76: L1668 1270/900 18 M

531 Base angle. Light brown both faces. Fabric: G. (not illustrated).
76: L1715 1275.5/905.5 6 N

532 Base angle. Light brown externally, grey to brown internally. Fabric: 1 S Sh; G. (not illustrated).
76: L1564 1275.5/905.5 6 I

533 Base angle. Light brown externally, grey internally. Fabric: 2 S Sh; G. (not illustrated).
76: L1535 β41 6

534 Base angle. Light brown externally, greyish brown internally. Fabric: 1 M Sh; G. (not illustrated).
76: L2202 1270/900 20 I

535 Base angle. Greyish brown externally, brown internally. Fabric: 1 S Sh; G. (not illustrated).
75: L1312 1270/900 14 B

536 Base angle. Greyish brown externally, grey internally. Fabric: G. (not illustrated).
75: L1400 1270/900 18 B

537 Base angle. Light brown externally, grey internally. Fabric: 1 M F; 1 M Sh; G. (not illustrated).
76: L1575 1275.5/905.5 6 K

538 Base angle. Greyish brown both faces. Fabric: 1 M Sh; G. (not illustrated).
75: L1181 1275.5/905.5 5 F

539 Base angle. Light brown both faces. Fabric: 1 S Sh; G. (not illustrated).
76: L1575 1275.5/905.5 6 K

540 Base angle. Light brown externally, grey internally. Fabric: 1 S Sh; G. (not illustrated).
76: L1539 β42 6

541 Base angle. Light brown both faces. Fabric: 1 S Sh; G. (not illustrated)
76: L1620 β43 6

542 Base angle. Light brown externally, grey internally. Fabric: 1 L F; 1 S Sh; G. (not illustrated).
76: L1576 1275.5/905.5 4 M

543 Base angle. Light brown externally, grey internally. Fabric: G. (not illustrated).
76: L1656 1270/900 13 D

544 Base angle. Greyish brown both faces. Fabric: G. (not illustrated).
75: L1396 1270/900 18 M

545 Base angle. Light brown externally, grey internally. Fabric: 1 S Sh; G. (not illustrated).
76: L1564 1275.5/905.5 6 I

546 Base angle. Brown externally, grey internally. Fabric: 1 S Sh; G. (not illustrated).
75: L1158 1275.5/905.5 4 G

547 Base angle. Light brown externally, grey internally. Fabric: 1 S Sh; G. (not illustrated).
75: L1202 1270/900 13 N

548 Base angle. Light brown to grey externally, greyish brown internally. Fabric: 1 M Sh; 1 L F. (not illustrated).
76: L1721 1270/900 18 I

549 Base angle. Light brown both faces. Fabric: 1 S Sh; G. (not illustrated).
76: L1576 1275.5/905.5 4 M

550 2 base angles joining. Brown externally, internal surface lost. Fabric: 1 S F; 1 S Sh. (not illustrated).
75: L1011 1270.5/905.5 Topsoil.

551 Base angle. Light brown externally, dark grey internally. Fabric: 1 L F. (not illustrated).
76: L1899 1270/900 19a H

552 Wall sherd. Brown both faces. Perforation made through the wall before firing. Fabric: 1 S Sh. (not illustrated).
76: L1552 1275.5/905.5 6 E

553 2 joining base sherds. Brown both faces. Perforation through the base made before firing. Fabric: 2 M F. (not illustrated).
75: L1469 1325.5/970.5 7 Feature 2

554 ? lid. Greyish brown externally, brown internally. Fabric: 1 M Sh; S. (not illustrated).
74: L203 1270.5/900.5 3

555 ? leg/handle. Light brown. Fabric: G. (not illustrated).
76: L2009 β43 6

OTHER CONTEXTS

556 Undecorated rim sherd. Light brown both faces with grey core. Fabric: 3 S F. Peake (1917) 434.
Floor 15 Norwich 63.948

557 Undecorated rim sherd. Light brown both faces with grey core. Fabric: G. Peake (1917) 434.
Floor 15 Norwich 63.948

558 Undecorated rim sherd. Light brown both faces. Fabric: 1 S F. Peake (1917) 434, fig. 89B.
Floor 15 Norwich 63.948

559 Rim sherd. Grey externally, light brown to grey internally. Decoration: On the rim, diagonal incised lines.
Fabric: 2 M Sh. Rim diam. 32cm.
Floor 16 Hearth 2′6″ down, B.M. Armstrong Coll.

560 Rim sherd. Brown both faces. Decoration: On top of the rim, finger tip impressions. Beneath the rim, a row of perforations made before firing. On the body beneath, irregularly scored incised lattice. Fabric: 2 M F. Peake (1917) 434, fig. 89F.
Floor 16 Norwich 63.948

561 Rim sherd. Light brown both faces with grey core. Decoration: A row of diagonal finger-nail impressions beneath the rim. Fabric: 2 M F. Peake (1917) 434, fig. 89A; Gibson (1982), 420 fig. GR1.3.
Floor 16 Norwich 63.948

562 Vessel. Brown to grey externally, internally grey. Decoration: On the rim, incised chevrons. Rim diam. 11.3cm.
Floor 16 Upper level Norwich 63.948

563 Rim sherd. light brown both faces with grey core. Decoration: On the external rim edge, lightly incised short diagonal lines. Fabric: nil.
Floor 16 Norwich 63.948

564 Rim sherd. Grey both faces. Decoration: On the outer edge of the rim, diagonal strokes. Fabric: 2 M F. Floor 16 B.M. Armstrong Coll.

565 Rim sherd. Light brown both faces with grey core. Decoration: On the rim, remains of transverse ? fingernail impressions. A row of perforations made before firing below the rim. Fabric: G.
Floor 16 Norwich 63.948

566 Rim sherd. Brown externally, grey internally. A perforation made before firing below the rim. Fabric: 1 M F.
Floor 42A Norwich 63.948

567 Wall sherd. Brown to grey externally, grey internally. Decoration: On the shoulder cordon, a row of finger-tip impressions. Fabric: 3 L F.
Floor 79 Norwich 63.948

568 Undecorated rim. Grey externally, grey to brown internally. Fabric: Nil.
Floor 80 Norwich 63.948

569 Undecorated rim. Brown externally, grey internally.
Floor 85A B.M. Armstrong Coll.

570 Undecorated base angle. Brown.
Floor 85A B.M. Armstrong Coll.

571 Undecorated rim. Grey externally, grey to brown internally.
Floor 85A B.M. Armstrong Coll.

572 Undecorated base angle. Brown externally, grey internally.
Floor 85C B.M. Armstrong Coll.

573 Undecorated rim. Grey to brown externally, light brown internally, with grey core. Fabric: 2 S F; 1 M Sh.
Floor 86 Norwich 63.948

574 Rim sherd. Brown both faces. Decoration: On the rim, indefinite transverse impressions. Fabric: 1 S Sh; G.
Kent's Low Floor. B.M. Armstrong Coll.

575 Undecorated rim. Light brown both faces. Fabric: 1 S F.
Kent's Low Floor. B.M. Armstrong Coll.

576 3 rim sherds. Brown externally, brown to grey internally. Decoration: On top of the rim, transverse to diagonal finger-tip impressions. Fabric: 2 M F.
Section SW of Black Hole. B.M. Armstrong Coll.

577 Wall sherd, brown externally, grey internally. Decoration: On the shoulder cordon, finger tip impressions.
Section SW of Black Hole. BM Armstrong Coll.

578 Wall sherd. Brown externally, grey internally. Perforation made before firing through the wall.
Section SW of Black Hole. B.M. Armstrong Coll.

579 Rim sherd. Grey throughout. A row of perforations made before firing in the neck. Fabric: 1 M F.
Hearth in pit near midden. N. of Floor 15. (=Pit 3) Norwich 63.948

Loom Weights

L1 Fragment from lower part of loom weight. Brown. Diam. of vertical perf: c 1.6cm. Kent's Low Floor. B.M. Armstrong Coll.

L2 Fragment from upper part of loom weight. Grey. Diam. of vertical perf: 2.3cm.
Black Hole 5F2. B.M. Armstrong Coll.

L3 Fragments (joining) of loom weight. Brown. Diam. of vertical perf. c1.5cm.
B.M. 76 L1519 & L1520 1275.5/905.5 6J

L4 Fragment from lower part of loom weight. Light brown. Diam. of vertical perf. 1.4cm.
Black Hole 5F5 B.M. Armstrong Coll.

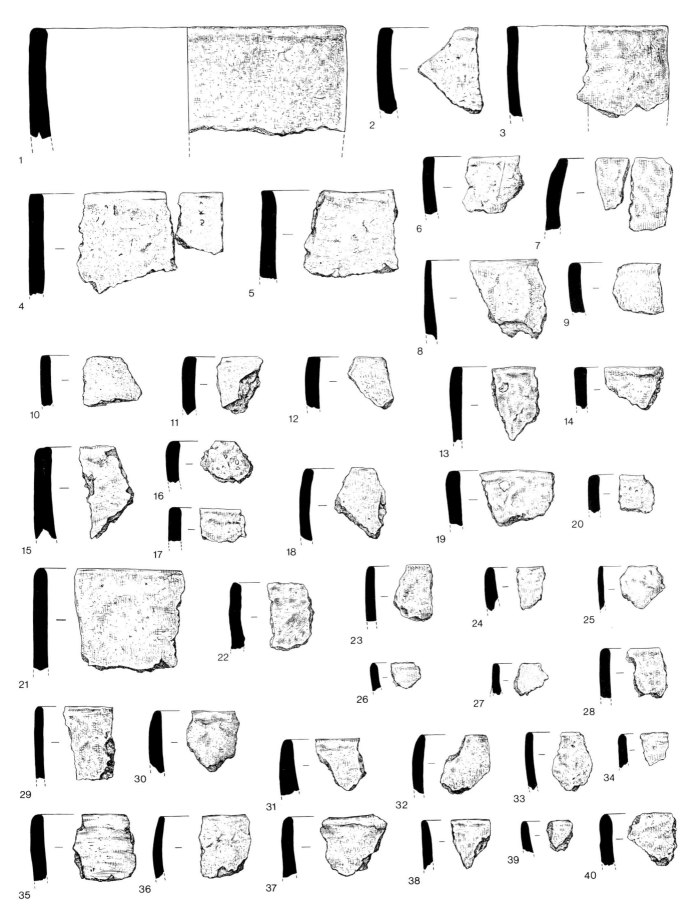

fig. 23   Bronze Age Bucket-shaped pottery from the Black Hole: *1-40*.

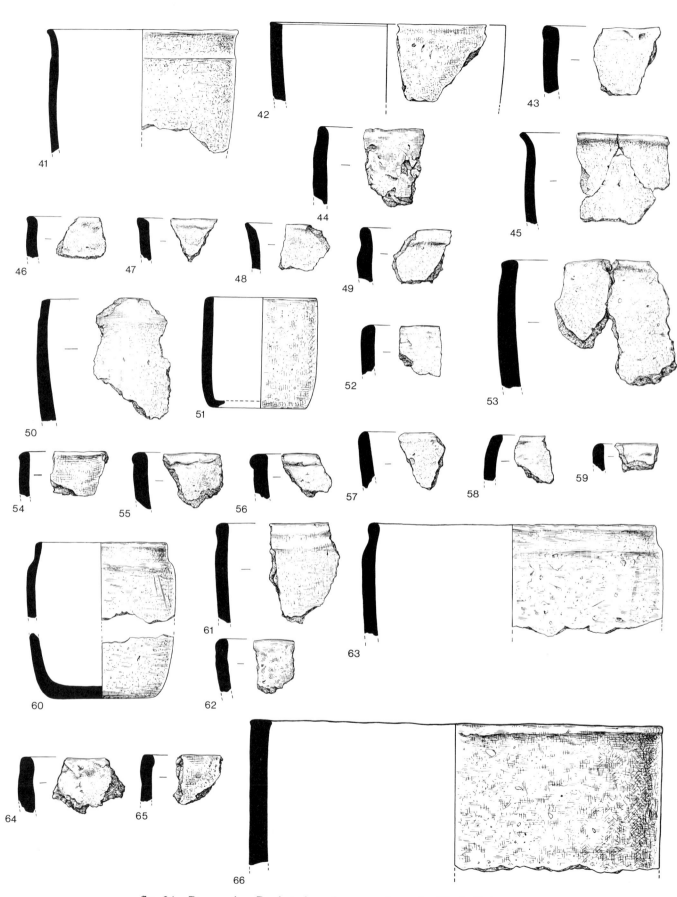

fig. 24   Bronze Age Bucket-shaped pottery from the Black Hole: *41-66.*

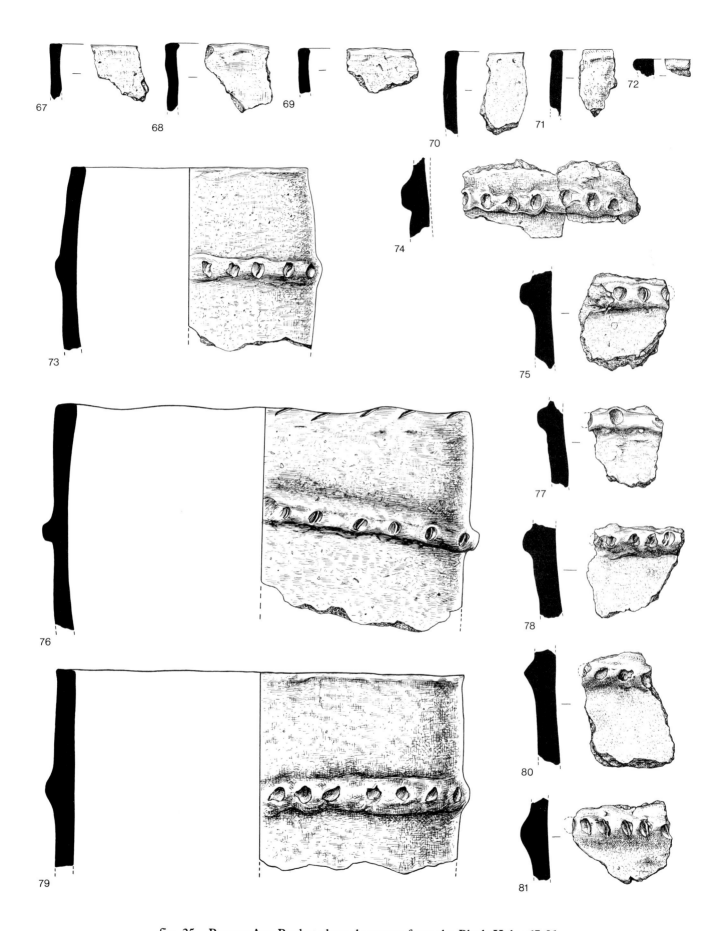

fig. 25   Bronze Age Bucket-shaped pottery from the Black Hole: *67-81*.

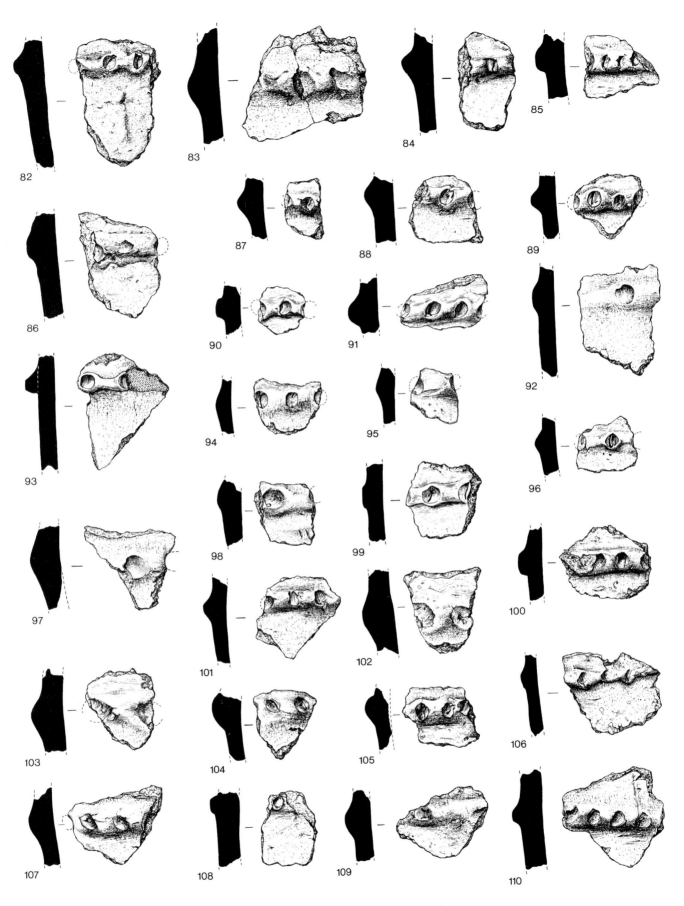

fig. 26 Bronze Age Bucket-shaped pottery from the Black Hole: *82-110*.

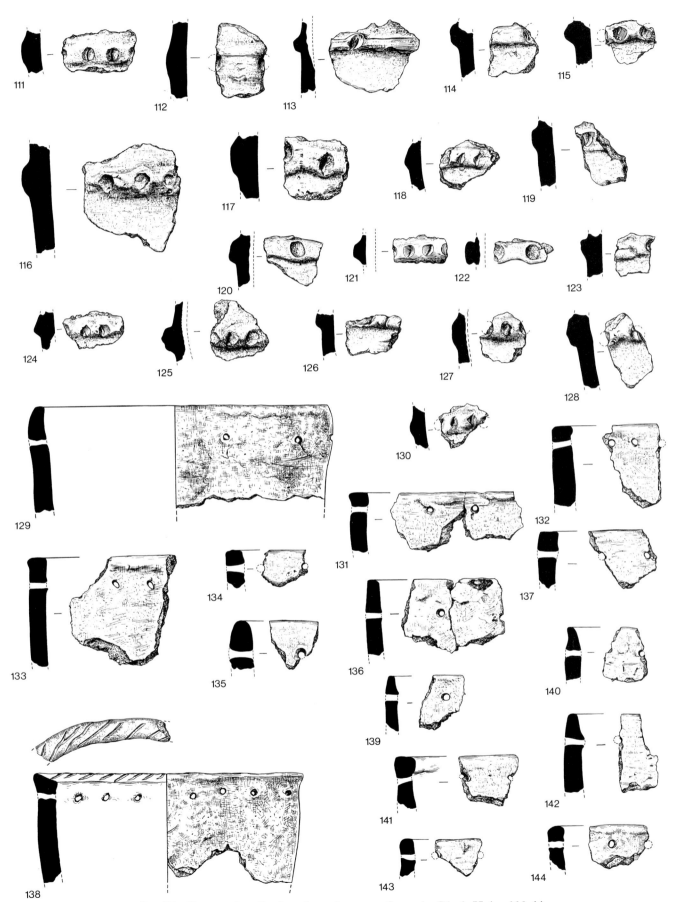

fig. 27   Bronze Age Bucket-shaped pottery from the Black Hole: *111-44*.

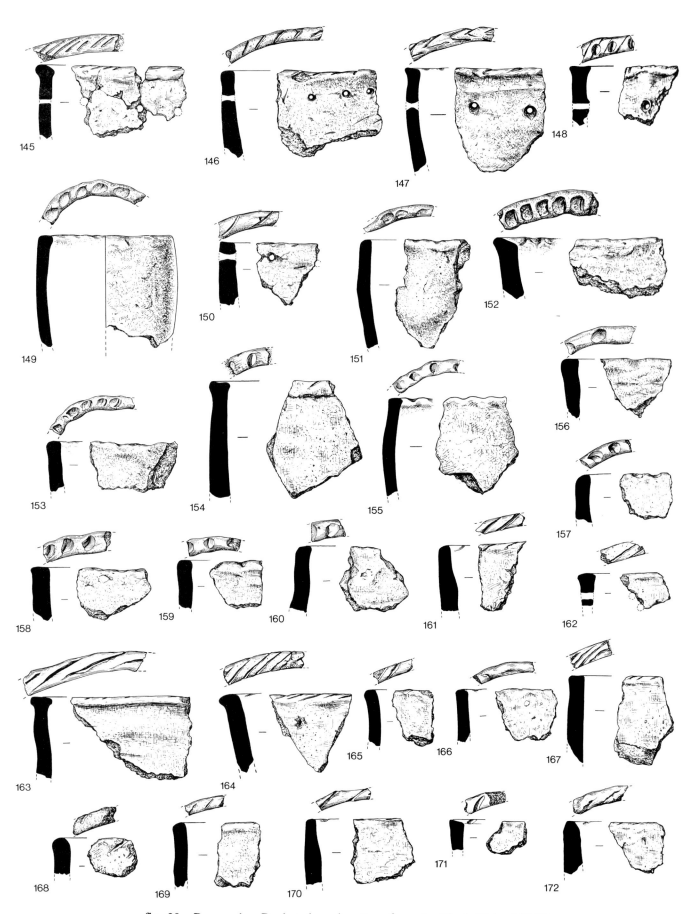

fig. 28   Bronze Age Bucket-shaped pottery from the Black Hole: *145-72.*

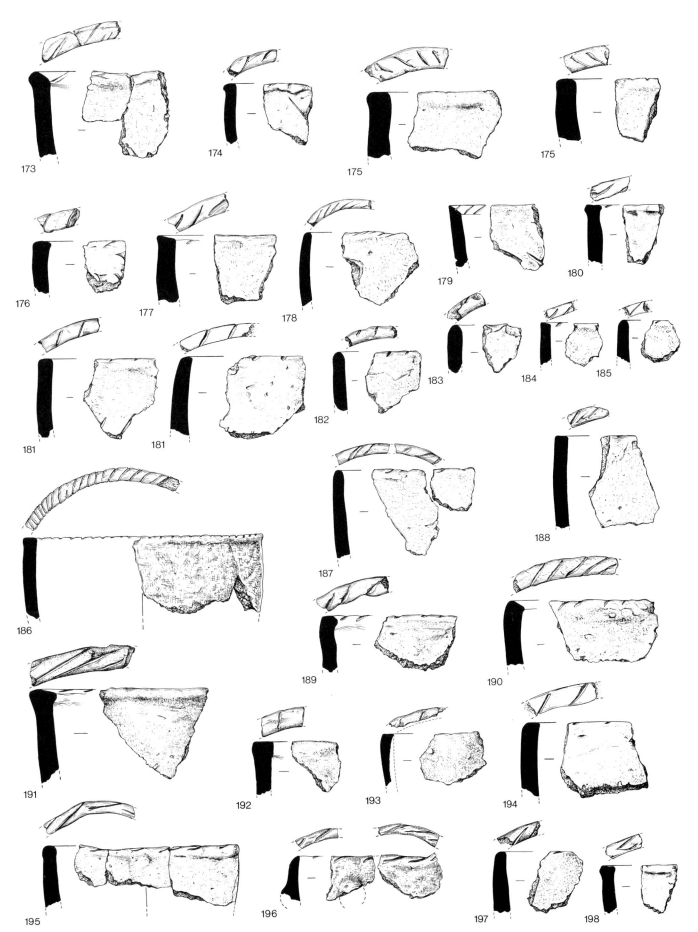

fig. 29   Bronze Age Bucket-shaped pottery from the Black Hole: *173-98*.

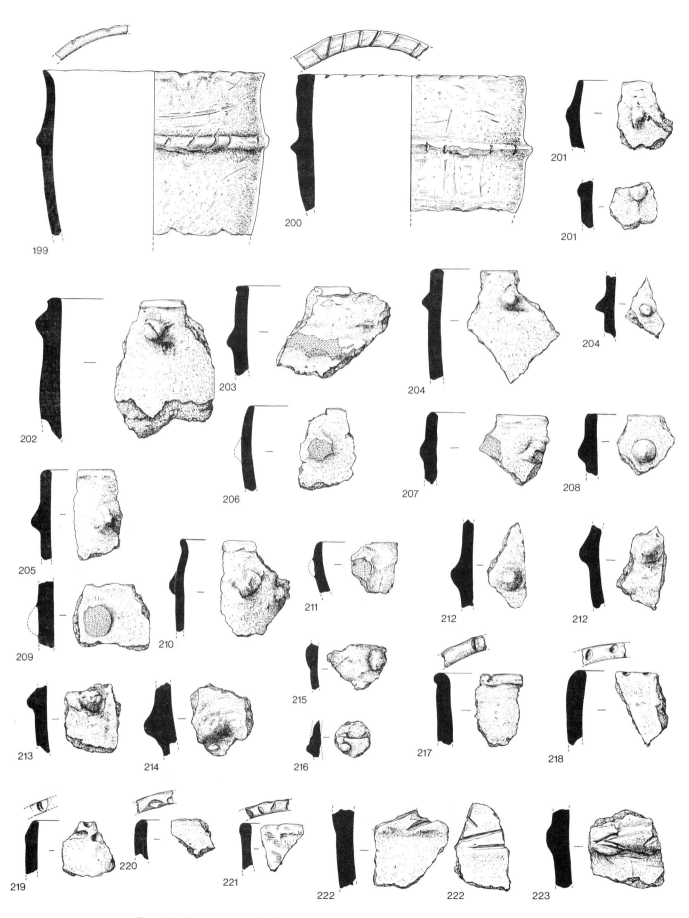

fig. 30   Bronze Age Bucket-shaped pottery from the Black Hole: *199-223*.

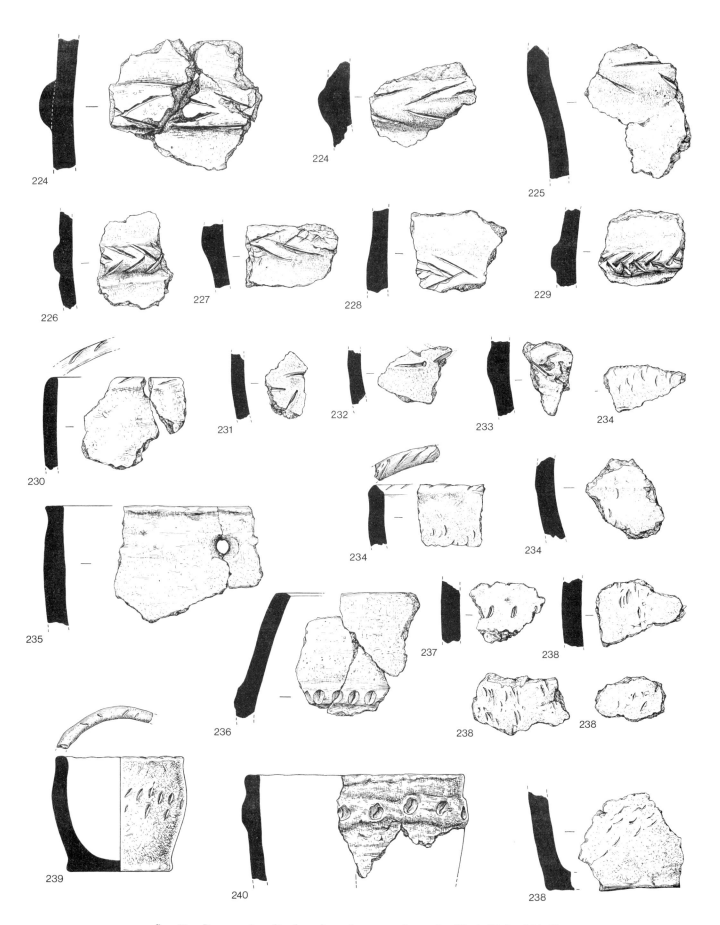

fig. 31   Bronze Age Bucket-shaped pottery from the Black Hole: *224-40*.

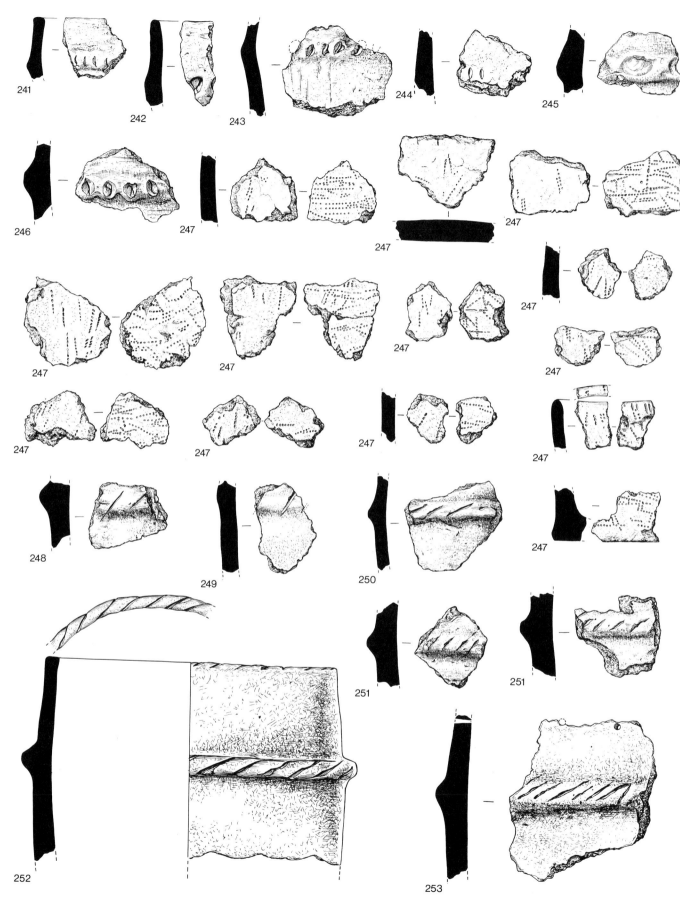

fig. 32 Bronze Age Bucket-shaped pottery from the Black Hole: *241-53*.

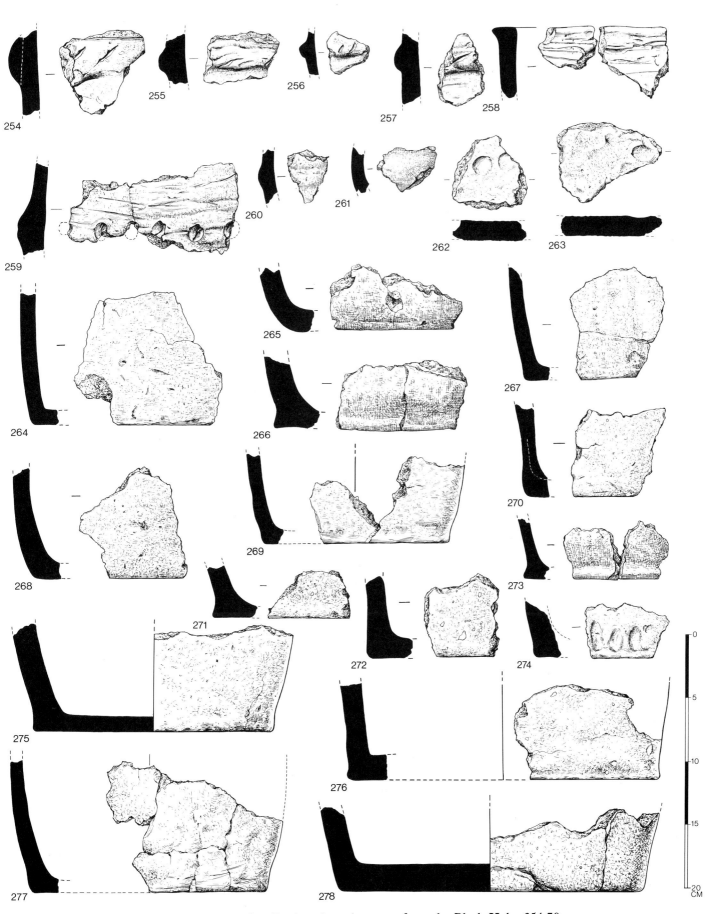

fig. 33   Bronze Age Bucket-shaped pottery from the Black Hole: *254-78*.

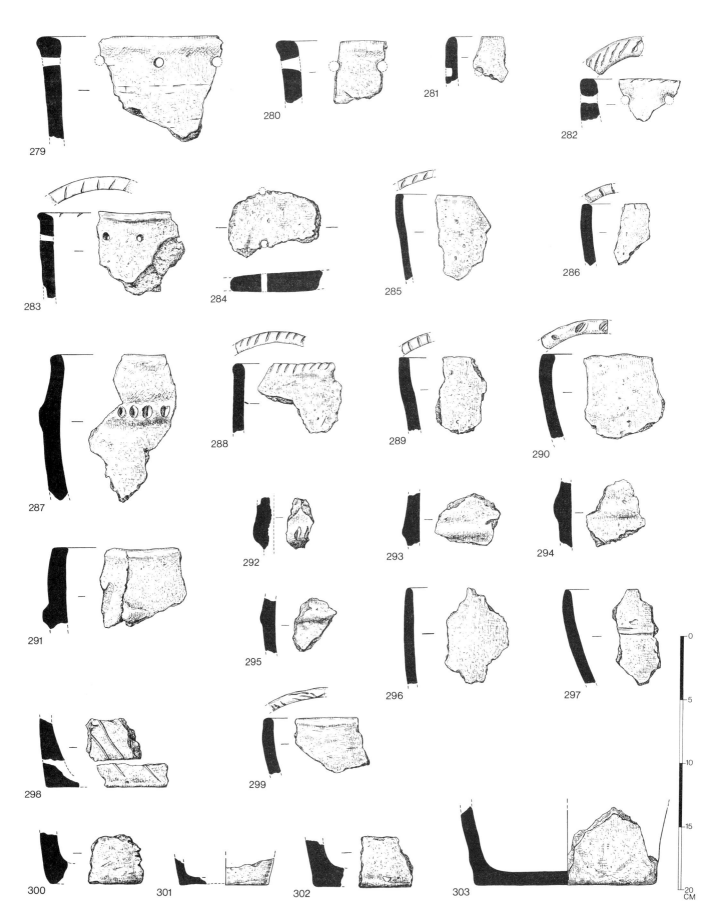

fig. 34   Bronze Age Bucket-shaped pottery from Section 7: *279-303*.

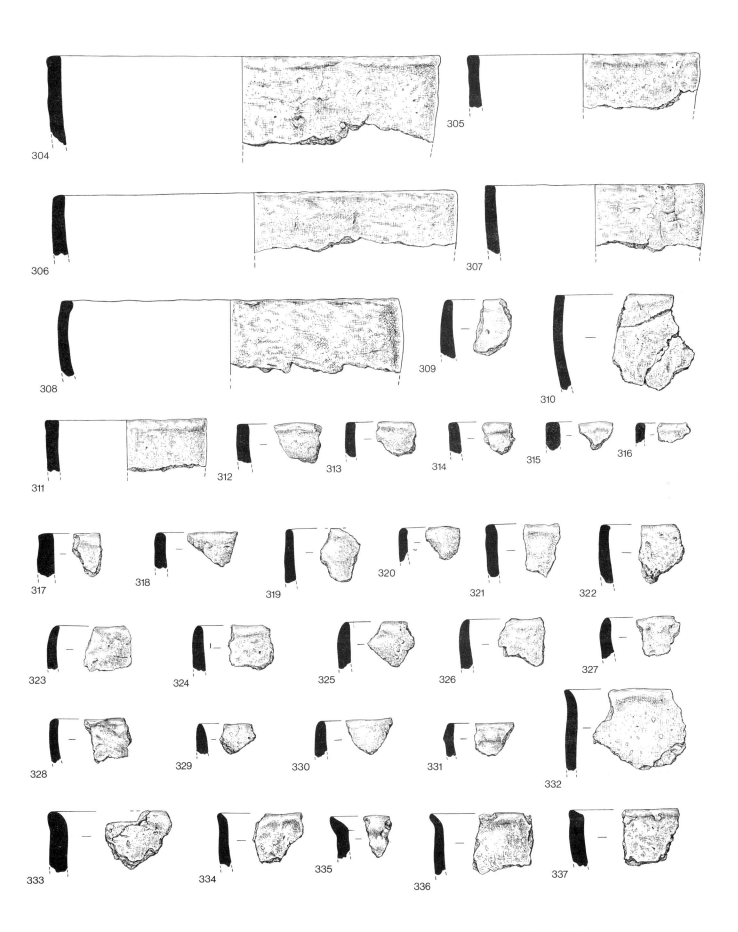

fig. 35   Bronze Age Bucket-shaped pottery from Shaft X and Area C: *304-37*

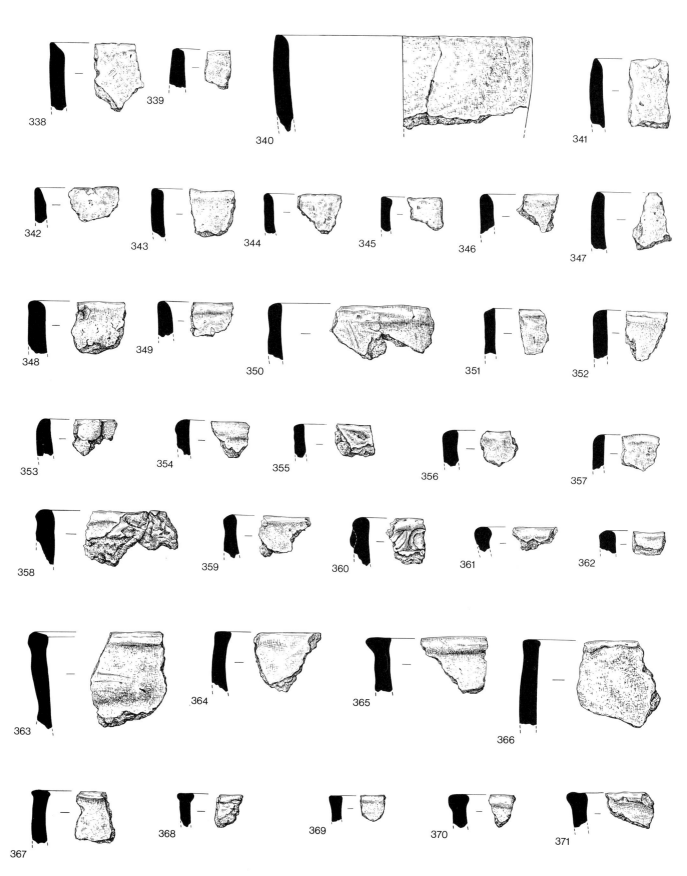

fig. 36   Bronze Age Bucket-shaped pottery from Shaft X and Area A: *338-71*.

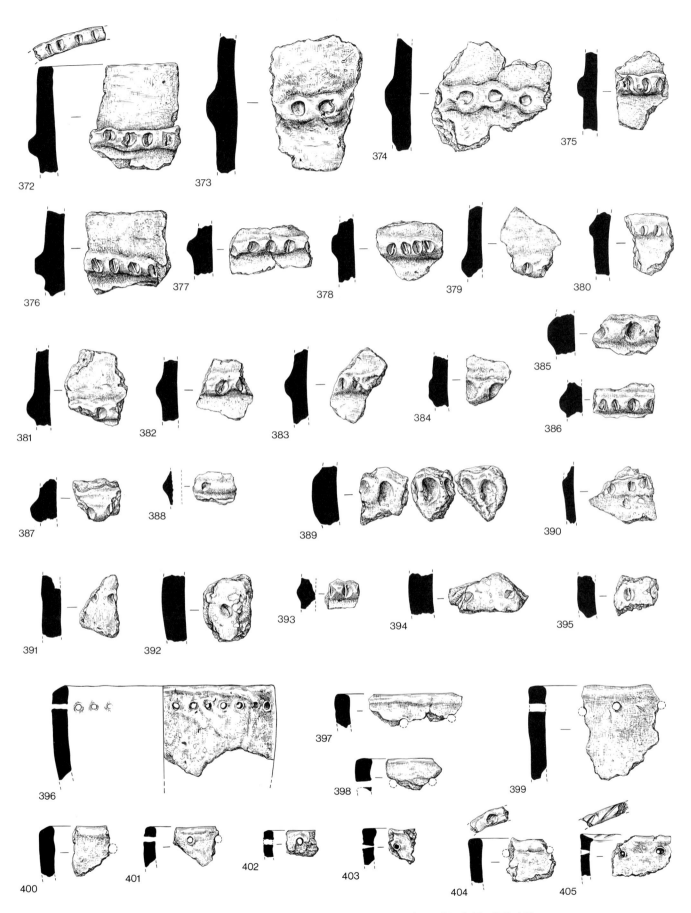

fig. 37 Bronze Age Bucket-shaped pottery from Shaft X: *372-405*.

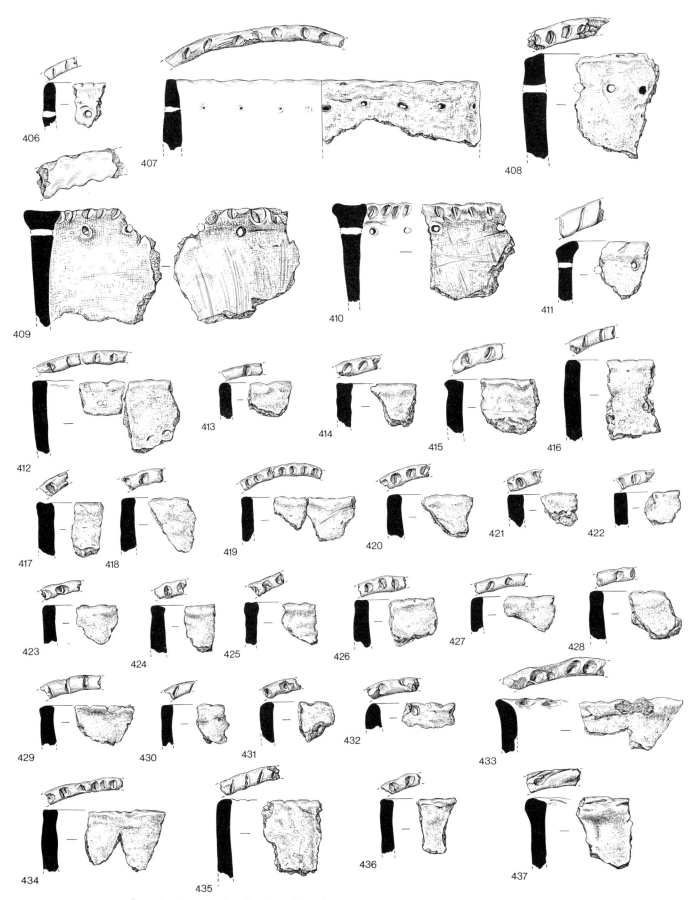

fig. 38 Bronze Age Bucket-shaped pottery from Shaft X and Area A: *406-37*.

406
407
408
409
410
411
412
413
414
415
416
417
418
419
420
421
422
423
424
425
426
427
428
429
430
431
432
433
434
435
436
437

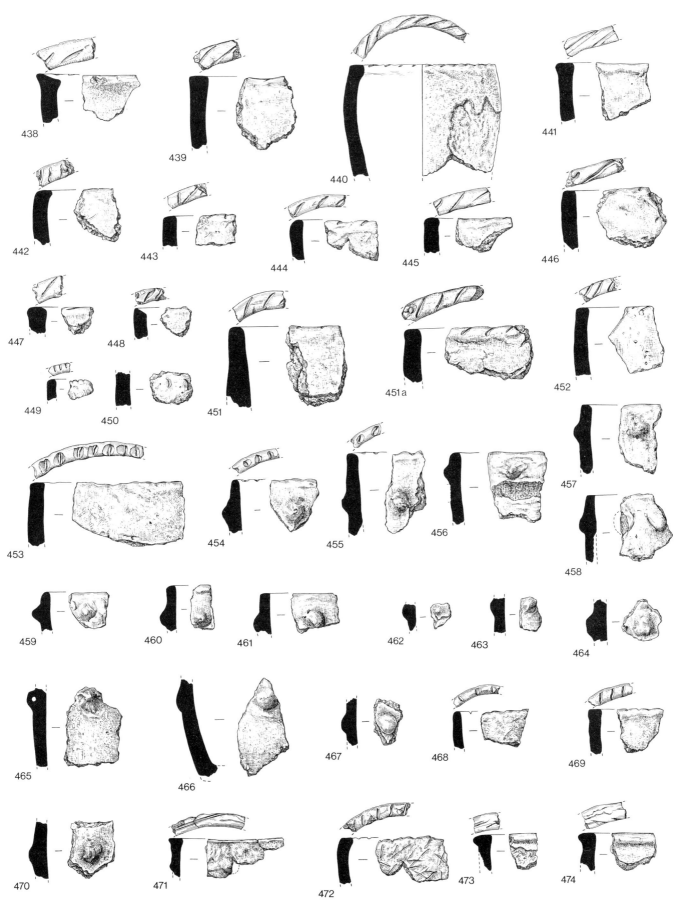

fig. 39   Bronze Age Bucket-shaped pottery from Shaft X and Area C: *438-74*.

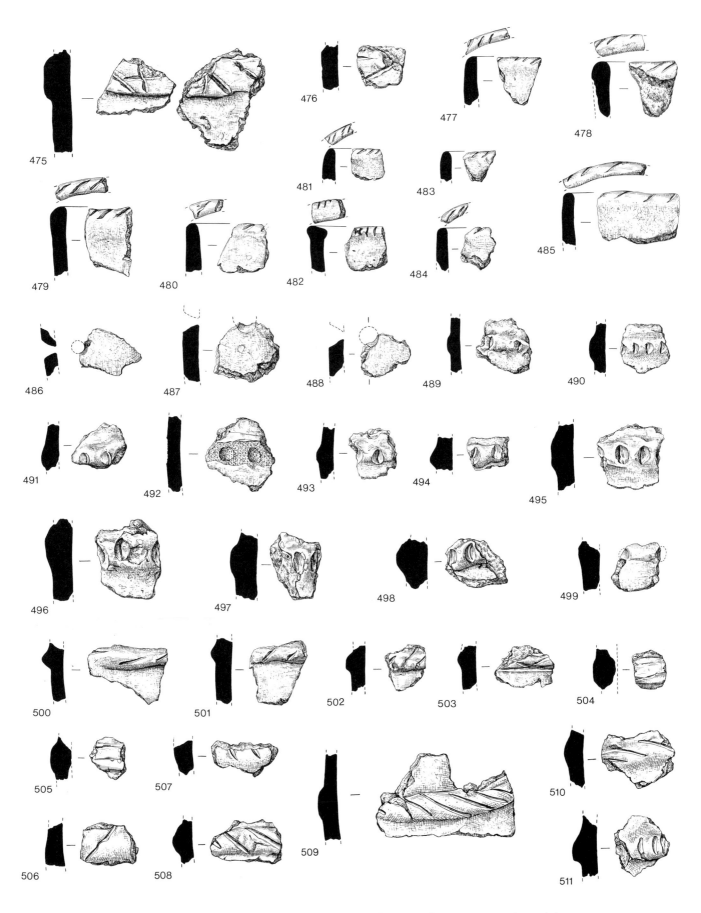

fig. 40   Bronze Age Bucket-shaped pottery from Shaft X and Area C: *475-511*.

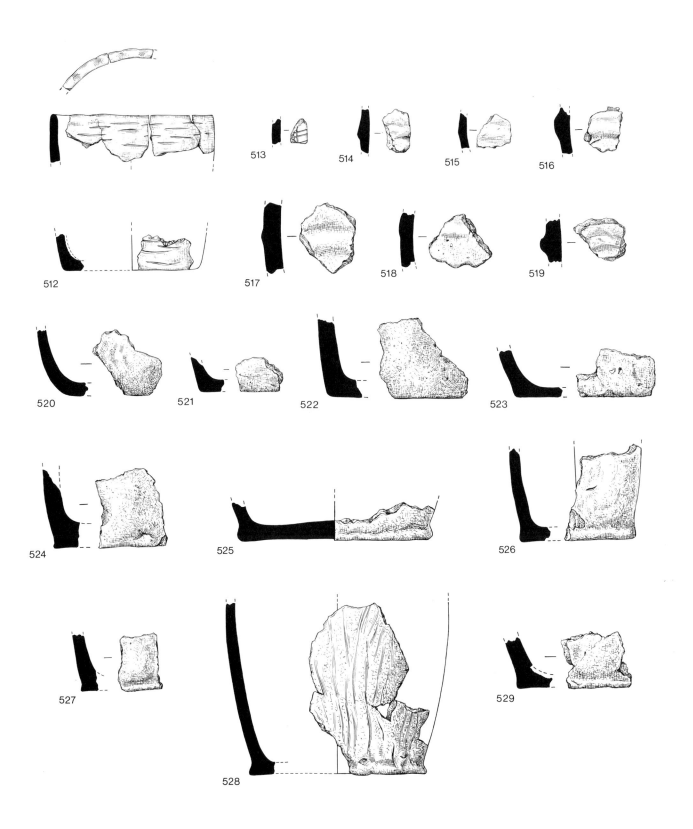

fig. 41   Bronze Age Bucket-shaped pottery from Shaft X: *512-29*.

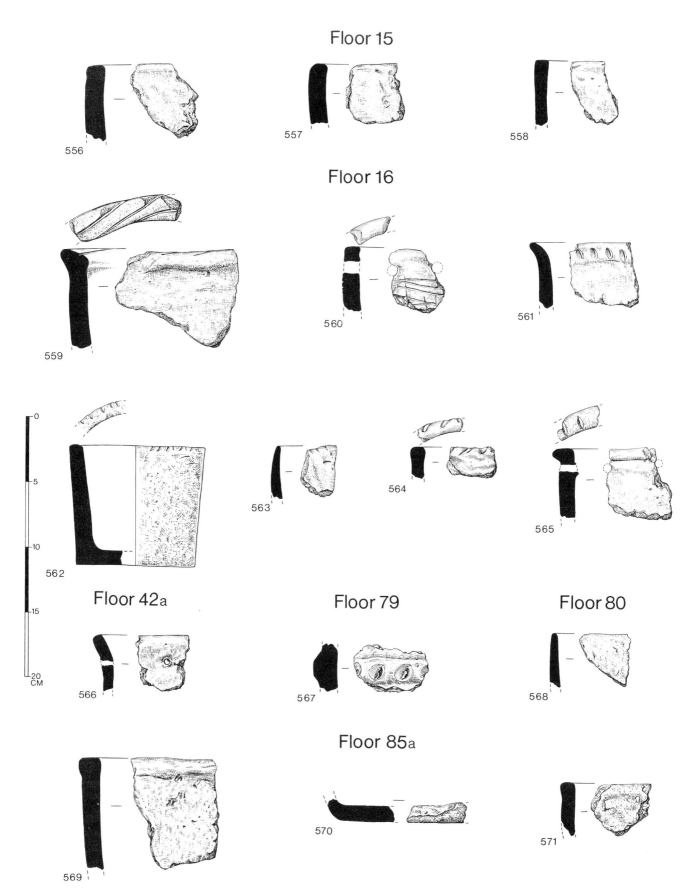

Floor 15

556 557 558

Floor 16

559 560 561

562 563 564 565

Floor 42a   Floor 79   Floor 80

566 567 568

Floor 85a

569 570 571

fig. 42   Bronze Age Bucket-shaped pottery from Floors 15, 16, 42A, 79, 80 & 85A: *556-71*.

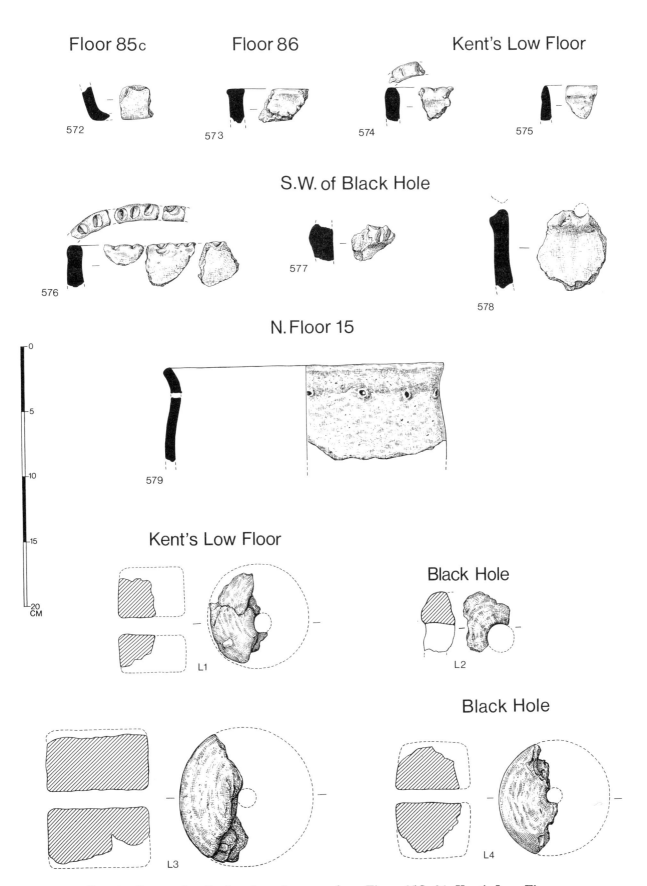

Floor 85c

Floor 86

Kent's Low Floor

572

573

574

575

S.W. of Black Hole

576

577

578

N. Floor 15

0

5

10

15

20
CM

579

Kent's Low Floor

L1

Black Hole

L2

Black Hole

L3

L4

fig. 43 Bronze Age Bucket-shaped pottery from Floors 85C, 86, Kent's Low Floor, Section SW of the Black Hole, Pit 3: *572-579* and Loomweights L1-4.

IV The Late Prehistoric, Roman and Later Wares

VALERY RIGBY

Apart from the Roman and post-Roman sherds, 119 sherds from the 1972-1976 excavations and 106 sherds from other collections, representing less than 1% of the total pottery assemblage, were set aside during processing from the main body of Bronze Age pottery. More than half lacked any typological characteristics, being small, and considerably worn body sherds. The combination of wall-thickness and fabric-texture - tempering and finish - set them apart from the bucket-shaped vessels of Bronze Age date. The vessel walls were thinner and the fabrics harder and more abrasive in texture, with flint, shell, sand and grog as temper, temper size was finer, and density less. Solely on the character of their fabrics, therefore, these sherds were assumed to belong to the first millennium BC and were added to the very few typologically secure, later L.B.A. and I.A. sherds, and designated as the late Prehistoric Pottery.

A selected group of 30 sherds was subjected to thin-section analysis by Dr I.C. Freestone of the British Museum Research Laboratory, with the aim of establishing whether or not the petrographic evidence supported the division of Bronze Age from late Prehistoric material. Dr Freestone reports:

'Thin sections were prepared from some thirty sherds and examined with a petrographic microscope.

The sherds may be grouped on the basis of five petrographic attributes, viz. (1) the presence of fine-grained calcite in the matrix and the presence and relative concentration of (2) quartz sand, (3) calcite fragments (greater than 0.06mm) and (4) grog and (5) flint temper. These characteristics are summarised in Table 11. The major sub-divisions of the pottery by fabric show a good correspondence with chronology. The earlier second millennium BC fabrics are characterised by the presence of sparse to abundant calcite fragments up to 1mm or so in diameter, usually shell but sometimes also chalk. On the whole the calcite fragments appear to be naturally included in the clay. These fabrics may be further sub-divided according to tempering material, whether grog (which in itself may contain shell), flint or coarse, millimeter-sized shell (possibly added deliberately in a few cases), or a mixture of shell or grog with flint; the subdivisions are indicated by spacing in Table 11, but their significance is not clear. The earlier fabrics contain a certain amount of quartz sand, but this is typically sparse.

The later fabrics are, in general, more sandy and lack fragmental calcite, although a few sherds contain minor fine-grained calcite in the matrix. These differences can be seen clearly in Table 11. They also contain grog and/or flint temper.

The properties of the earlier calcite-rich pastes are likely to have differed significantly from the later pastes with minor or no calcite, particularly in their behaviour during and after firing, where care would be required not to over fire.'

Petrographic analysis has therefore supported the division into Bronze Age and late Prehistoric groups originally based upon typology and the superficial characteristics of the fabrics. It demonstrates that although they were supplying settlements in the same locality, the earlier and later potters chose different clays and somewhat different tempering agents. The former preferred the shelly calcareous clays which could be found in the Fen deposits, about 10km. west of Grimes Graves, beyond the edge of the Chalk. In addition, they probably also used superficial clays overlying and derived from the chalk in which fragmental chalk was naturally present. In contrast,

TABLE 11: comparison of the principal petrographic features of the earlier and later prehistoric pottery

Cat No/ (Inventory No.)	Matrix Calcite	Fragmental Calcite	Quartz Sand	Grog Temper	Flint Temper
73	1	1	1	2	?1
138	1	2	1	2	-
230	1	2	1	2	-
247	1	1	1	1	?1
251	1	2	1	2	-
252	1	1	1	1	-
258	1	1	1	2	-
311	1	1	1	1	-
407	1	1	1	2	-
469	1	2	1	2	-
3	1	2	1	2	1
4	1	1	1	2	2
49	1	1	1	2	2
60	1	2	1	2	2
150	1	1	1/2	1	1
389	1	2	2	-	-
433	1	2	2	-	-
236	1	2	1	-	2
310	1	1	1	-	2
410	1	1	1	-	2
(L1880)	1	1	1	-	2
LP5	1	-	2	-	2
LP6	1	-	2	-	2
(L1627)	-	-	1/2	2	-
(L2144)	-	-	2	2	-
LP7	-	-	2	-	2
(L1123)	-	-	2	-	1
(L1878)	-	-	1	-	2
LP10	-	-	2	1	?1

(Left margin vertical labels: **EARLY**, **GROUP**, **LATE GROUP**)

Key: 1 = present/minor constituent
    2 = common/abundant, major constituent

Abundance of calcite in matrix not estimated, presence/absence only recorded

——   Indicates sub-groups within major division

the later potters preferred non-calcareous clay deposits which would be present in remnants of Boulder Clay and other superficial deposits overlying the Chalk. Each group may have developed rather different potting techniques, for their pastes would have had different handling properties. The strong preference of the early potters for highly calcareous pastes must have presented a firing problem because shell begins to break down at around 750C, when carbon dioxide is produced, such a temperature being easily achievable in a bonfire, on a fine day, with dry fuel. Clearly some Bronze Age potters had to aim for a low firing temperature, and vessel size and wall thickness could have been critical in the process, comparatively large size and thick walls helping to reduce the temperature achieved. By avoiding shell, and hence the disruptive spalling effects of the carbon dioxide it releases when heated, and relying upon more stable quartz and flint temper, the later prehistoric potters did not face such an acute problem of firing temperature leading to the development of thinner walled vessels, and a much wider range of sizes.

Typologically later sherds have indeed been shown to be petrographically different to the bucket-shaped vessels. The abundant shell of the latter, both as temper and shelly clay matrices almost disappears while sandy clays, flint and grog survive. This result suggests that otherwise undiagnostic, sandy textured flint - and grog-tempered body sherds should be later in date.

Superficially, the late Prehistoric sherds represent a period from the Late Bronze Age to the Late Iron Age. However, when compared to the number and condition of the earlier bucket-shaped vessels, these sherds form a group too small and too obviously weathered, residual and redeposited to be interpreted as evidence for continuous occupation in the immediate area. The sherds have clearly enjoyed a long, varied and mobile history since their vessels were first smashed or discarded. It is quite possible that these later Prehistoric sherds, along with the Roman and later wares discussed below, were introduced from some distance when they were already markedly residual, not generated by settlement, but the product of later agricultural processes. Moreover such small and light-weight sherds are so easily intruded by a variety of natural and human agencies into apparently securely stratified contexts on open rural sites, that any chronological evidence they provide has to be used with the utmost caution.

One pot from Shaft X, two from the 'Black Hole' and one from the area south-west of the 'Black Hole' require separate consideration because each is represented by more than 20 sherds, all in good condition and with numerous joins (*LP. 1, 5, 7 & 9*). Their condition suggests that they should be contemporary with the bucket-shaped vessels, but typologically and technologically they stand apart, and should be later in date. In the case of two pots (*LP5 & LP7*), sherds from rim, body and base areas were recovered by Armstrong, and although they cannot be repaired to give complete profiles, there are sufficient joins for profiles to be restored in the illustrations. When restored, the sherds from Shaft X (*LP1*) comprise approximately a half circuit about 9cm deep from the lower body of a large jar. In the absence of base, upper body or rim sherds, it is likely that there was only a single large sherd, or no more than three or four adjoining, which suffered further fragmentation during transport to and final deposition in Shaft X. Clearly these vessels have had a different history of breakage, dispersal and redeposition from that of the single, small, miscellaneous late Prehistoric sherds. While they, and also pot *LP9*, may be rubbish generated by Iron Age occupation in the immediate vicinity, they are still sufficiently fragmentary to have been introduced during agricultural operations from a place of discard at some remove from the site.

The Fabrics

All fabric identifications were made using the hand specimen, followed up by a selective programme of thin-section analysis. The initial processing had separated out a limited range of related wares with the result that the main categories are limited to flint-, sand- and grog- tempered wares, with little or no shell, see Table 12.

Flint-tempered wares

In all, 26 rims, 4 bases and 173 body sherds were identified, making it by far the largest fabric category. The matrix is normally non-calcareous and rather sandy in texture, either because a natural sandy clay was used, or because sand was added as additional temper to a fine-grained clay. There is considerable variety in the size and density of the calcined flint temper, from fine to coarse inclusion size, and from sparse to dense frequency.

Some sherds include only a limited range of grit sizes perhaps suggesting that the temper was sorted or sieved during preparation. They represent mainly thin-walled and burnished 'fine' ware vessels. Burnishing is a process of tooling and smoothing used

TABLE 12   Inventory of late Prehistoric sherds by fabric.

Fabrics 1972-6 Excavations	Burnished 'Fine'			Unfinished 'Coarse'		
	Rim	Base	Sherds	Rim	Base	Sherds
Flint	2	0	20	4	2	39
LP1	-	-	-	0	0	40
Sub-total	2	0	20	4	2	79
Grog	0	0	2	1	1	8
Sand	1	0	1	0	0	3
Organic/Dung	0	0	1	0	0	3
Vesicular				0	0	1
Total	3	0	24	5	3	94
Armstrong Collection						
Flint						
LP9	8	0	12			
Black Hole						
LP7	10	1	29			
LP5	-	-	-	6	1	33
LP6	1	0	0			
Others	1	0	0			
Total flint	20	1	41	6	1	33
Grog				1	0	0
Shell				1	0	0

to develop on the treated surface a layer of aligned fine clay particles, particularly mica flakes, which masks large inclusions and produces a comparatively impermeable glossy finish.

In other sherds, little or no sorting of the flint temper is apparent, for numerous large and angular grits protrude through the surfaces, no matter how well finished, and interfere with surface treatment.

Most examples of this 'random' grit size appear in sherds from 'coarse' vessels with unfinished surfaces rather than 'fine' burnished ones. They are more easily distinguishable when heavily tempered.

There are no identifiable examples of 'rough-cast' bases (with grits added to the underside of the base) so typical of the Late Bronze Age, and no deeply scored or combed sherds, typical of the Iron Age. Only the pot *LP1* exhibits a deliberately roughened finish on its outer surface, but this is executed with short, lightly incised scratch marks so that the amount of actual roughening was slight.

One necked and shouldered jar has an unusual faceted finish (*LP5*). The vessel itself was only roughly shaped, by an unskilled or careless potter, so that it is extremely uneven and asymmetrical in shape. No attempt was made to smooth out the inner surface, although time and effort had been expended upon the exterior. A flat, rather sharp-edged tool had been used like a trimming knife to produce narrow, glossy facets which left the surface uneven, yet successfully masked the flint temper. The trimmed or burnished facets are horizontal on the rim and shoulder and vertical on the lower body, an arrangement frequently used on pottery of Middle Iron Age date in southern Britain.

Only six sherds (5 pots) are decorated with finger-tip or finger-nail impressions. A small carinated jar, *LP3*, has low relief cabling on the top edge of the rim, produced with either finger nail or spatulate tool. There is a small body sherd from another carinated jar, not illustrated, with a row of fine, angled slashes along the carination (M72:149). Two rather shapeless jars each have a row of finger tip impressions on the shoulder and low relief cabling on the outer edge of the rim (*LP2*). Finally, a shouldered jar, *LP4*, has deep finger tip impressions on the inside edge of the rim.

The 'fine' burnished wares are plain, and the majority of sherds are too small and enigmatic for identification. Two tiny rims, neither illustrated, (75:L1125 from 1325.5/967.5 2 and from the Black Hole) may be from rimless rounded cups or bowls like examples from Staple Howe (Brewster 1963: fig. 42, 8-9), and Runnymede Bridge, Berkshire, (Longley 1980: fig. 37, 431). A larger rim sherd, *LP6*, appears to be a carinated bowl of a type represented at Darmsden, Suffolk (Cunliffe 1968: fig. 2, 15-9), and Chinnor, Oxfordshire (Richardson and Young 1951: fig. 49-50).

By far the most complete 'fine' burnished wares are a bead rimmed bowl, *LP7*, and a necked bowl, *LP9*, in fabrics which thin-section analysis groups together. Both are types which appear to be more at home in the later Iron Age, from perhaps the mid-fourth century B.C., for they occur at Little Waltham, Essex, forms 5 and 15 respectively (Drury 1978). However, since bead-rimmed vessels have been identified in much earlier assemblages, at Runnymede Bridge, Berkshire (Longley 1980: fig. 37, 422-7) and West Harling, Norfolk (Clarke & Fell 1953: fig. 15, 65), the chronological problem remains unresolved. The simple shape of the necked bowl is equally difficult to date for again there are examples from Runnymede Bridge (Longley 1980: fig. 31, 262-5). A third 'fine' ware form which appears to belong to the Middle or Late Iron Age is the globular jar with narrow everted rim *LP8*. It has not been thin-sectioned, but superficially the fabric appears identical to the bead-rimmed and necked jars, *LP7* and *LP9*. Typologically it is related to Little Waltham form 4, which occurs in various sand-tempered ware, and which has also been identified locally at Orsett (Hedges & Buckley 1978: fig. 43, 1).

Generally in southern Britain, flint-tempered pottery is characteristic of the first half of the first millennium BC. By the second half, it had been replaced by other tempering agents such as sand, shell, calcite and grog, depending upon local availability, or by the exploitation of geological, and more superficial, glauconite-rich clay deposits, which required no added temper. The trend was therefore away from hard, coarse and angular, white and obtrusive flint temper, to softer, finer textured and more easily camouflaged types, at a time when spare waste flint was presumably increasingly scarce. However, in at least one area of eastern England, Sturry in East Kent, the use of flint temper appears to have survived until the introduction of the fast wheel rendered it no longer feasible, and also too painful to the potter (Ince 1929: p.93-4). On the other side of the Thames Estuary at Little Waltham, Essex, the use of flint temper appears to have just about survived into the Middle Iron Age, although varying grades of quartz sand were already predominant by the third century B.C. (Drury 1978: p.56-8). Superficially at least, Grimes Graves is an obvious area where waste flint could have been readily available for use as temper into the Middle Iron Age.

Flint-tempered wares in Shaft X and the Black Hole

By sherd count, most of the flint-tempered sherds were found in these two features; all but a few of the remainder occurred in topsoil. The stratified exceptions, like for example, *LP1* and *LP3*, were associated with typical bucket-shaped vessels. This association is open to a number of different interpretations some of which raise questions about the sequence and chronology of the relevant features.

A distinction has to be made between sherds recovered from Shaft X in the 1972-6 excavations for which precise stratigraphical contexts are known and those in the Armstrong Collection (see p.27). The best and most deeply stratified example of flint-tempered ware is the jar of unknown form, *LP1*. It appears to have survived as a large sherd, in good condition, until further fragmentation occurred during its final deposition in the weathering cone of Shaft X (see p.31). Typologically undatable, temper and technique set it apart from the main bulk of the Bronze Age pottery recovered. Thin section analysis associates it with the bead-rimmed bowl, *LP7*, from the Armstrong Collection, and the jar with finger-tip decoration *LP2*. If similarity in fabric is indicative of similar potting techniques and hence similar manufacturing date, then the jar *LP1* could be five centuries later than the bucket-shaped vessels with which it was associated. Therefore, either *LP1* was introduced later into the earlier group of material, or the main Bronze Age assemblage is a residual group which was deposited with the later sherd.

Three typologically undistinguished sherds of 'fine' burnished ware 76:L1864 & L2144, sparsely tempered with fine flint grits, were found in Shaft X, (1270/900 layer 20a). In technique, they also appear more at home in the first millennium BC rather than in any earlier period. If this is the case, then together with *LP1*, they may indicate the uncertain date of deposition of the contexts in which they were found. Conversely, despite the technical differences, pot *LP1* and its accompanying 'fine' sherds may be con-temporary with the associated bucket urns, as their contexts indicate, representing an early stage in the transition from older to newer potting traditions at the turn of the second and first millennium BC.

Grog-tempered wares

Thirteen sherds tempered solely with grog, or with sparse to rare additional inclusions, have been identified. One sherd has traces of combing on the exterior, so it is presumably Late Iron Age or early Roman in date. The remainder are undiagnostic body sherds, two of which appear to be burnished 'fine' wares. Since all are from hand-made vessels, they should pre-date the mid-first century AD.

There is some evidence to suggest that grog was increasingly used as the main tempering agent for 'fine' wares at least from the 6th century BC onwards when the amount of added flint was being drastically reduced. However, at Little Waltham, Fabric E, the grog-tempered fabric, is absent from good Period II contexts which perhaps implies a date in the later Iron Age for its introduction there. At Grimes Graves itself, the only typologically diagnostic sherd in essentially grog tempered ware was the bead-rimmed jar, *LP10*, which still includes rare large flint chips.

One grog tempered sherd, with a burnished finish, was found associated with pot *LP1*, in Shaft X. As with the flint-tempered wares discussed above, its presence is open to widely differing interpretations.

Four sherds have coarse black inclusions and voids which suggest the use of organic (?dung) or vegetable matter. They are undatable and could easily be Dark Age in date.

Sand-tempered wares

Five sherds appear to be from handmade vessels in sand-tempered wares. There is one tiny rim (75:L1337 from 1325.5/970.5, Feature 2), probably from a necked bowl of Iron Age date (or less likely, an earlier biconical carinated bowl) with a glossy burnished finish inside and out. The remaining sherds are typologically undiagnostic body sherds found in unstratified contexts.

Catalogue

Late Prehistoric sherds

Where possible, sherds considered to be stratigraphically significant or typologically diagnostic have been illustrated. They have been arranged according to fabric type and finish, with the exception of pot *LP1* which, because of its stratigraphic significance, has been placed first.

Flint-tempered wares

LP1   Forty sherds from the same half circuit of the lower body of a jar of unknown form with no trace of any shaping for the base, shoulder or rim. The base must have been less than 16cm, the maximum girth greater than 21cm in diameter, and the height greater than 10cm. Built of overlapped and luted slabs of clay about 5cm wide and 0.6cm thick, little attempt had been made by the potter to smooth out on the outer surface the horizontal ridges produced by this technique.

The clay matrix is non-calcareous and contains silt grade quartz sand. It is moderately tempered with crushed calcined flint, possibly unsorted, for the grit size is random and extends to 0.8cm which is greater than the wall thickness. Before firing the interior surface was lightly brushed horizontally while the exterior was slightly roughened by means of short vertical scratchings. The exterior surface colour is a variegated reddish brown, the interior is black and soot encrusted. In the fracture, this discolouration can be seen to have penetrated deep into the wall, via pores in the clay matrix, but more notably via the air spaces around the temper. As a result, burning has produced a markedly wavy 'sandwich' line between the burnt interior and non-burnt exterior zones.
75:L1144, L1181, L1266, L1329, L1451; 76:L1739, L1810, L1871, L1878, L1880, L1895, L1901, L1903, L2215, L2355, L2358, L2507, L2571, L2590, L2595.

Shaft X 1270/900; Layers 14, 18, 19b&c, 20a, B-D, F-I and S; 1275.5/900.5 5F. There is also one sherd which is almost certainly from this vessel in the Armstrong Collection, from the Black Hole.

The sherds are all from the same part of the pot. A vertical and horizontal plot of their contexts within Shaft X shows that, with one exception, the sherds are concentrated in the same area of four contiguous layers, suggesting that they were dumped at the same time. Since there are numerous joins, it is possible that there was just a single large sherd which was fragmented further during its final deposition in Shaft X. In condition therefore, the vessel belongs with the bucket-shaped vessels with which it was stratigraphically associated, rather than with the individual, small worn typologically later prehistoric sherds found elsewhere on the site. Having undergone much the same history of use and discard as the Bronze Age bucket-shaped vessels, like them it could have been generated by a settlement in the immediate area, and that settlement may have been Bronze Age in date.

Despite its condition and context, in temper, texture, wall-thickness and finishing, the pot belongs to the traditions of the first millennium BC rather than that of the earlier bucket-shaped vessels. Thin-section analysis grouped its fabric with those of the bead-rimmed bowl, *LP7*, and a jar decorated with finger-tip impressions, *LP2*, which would place it at some chronological remove from the main bulk of Bronze Age pottery, and nearer to the middle of the first millennium BC. Given its stratigraphic position, such a late date would have a noticeable effect upon any *terminus post quem* for the deposition of the contents of Shaft X, to the full depth excavated. The bucket-shaped vessels, despite their number and condition, would therefore have been deposited in Shaft X, between three and six centuries after the initial discard of their latest types.

In the absence of any typological characteristics, pot *LP1* cannot be dated other than to suggest that it was in use some time between the eleventh and fourth centuries BC.

LP2   Two sherds from the same biconical carinated jar, decorated with a row of finger tip impressions on the shoulder and carefully worked cabling on the outer edge of the rim.
Sandy textured matrix with sparse to moderate temper, mainly less than 0.2cm in length, but with the occasional inclusion greater than 0.5cm. Grey ware, with worn poorly finished orange-buff exterior surface and unfinished and uneven interior surface.
74:L443 1325.5/970.5 (2 examples)
A rather shapeless jar with a narrow shoulder zone which may indicate that it was made at a later date in the period 8th to 6th centuries BC. There is also a sherd from a second larger example (75:L1123) found in the same feature.

LP3   A single rim sherd from a small carinated jar decorated with lightly impressed cabling on the top edge of the rim. Sandy textured matrix, with sparse flint temper mainly less than 0.2cm in length. Dark grey core; rather rough and unsmoothed surface.
74:L552. β 6 6 Chipping Floor CIII
A small version of the basic carinated jar shape typical of Site II at West Harling, Norfolk (Clark & Fell 1953: figs. 10-11), and apparently current 8th to 6th century BC.

LP4   A single rim sherd from a necked and shouldered jar with high relief cabling produced by finger tip impressions along the top edge of the rim. Heavily tempered with flint mainly below 0.2cm, but with occasional grits over 0.5cm. Grey core with brownish grey unfinished surfaces.
Norwich Museum Collection. Floor 16.
Probably to be dated to the same period as *LP5* below.

LP5   Over 40 sherds, rims, bases and body sherds, from a roughly shaped neck and shouldered jar with flattened rim top and splayed base. Noticeably coarse-grained sandy textured matrix with moderate flint temper, mainly below 0.2cm in length. In the section there is a thick dark grey core with thin orange margins and surfaces. Produced by an 'unskilled' potter; no attempt had been made to even out vertical and horizontal ridges and furrows, formed where

individual slabs overlapped, before finishing the pot. Using a technique akin to knife-trimming, the exterior surface was shaved and burnished into narrow, sharp facets, horizontal on the shoulder and vertical on the lower body. Most of the flint inclusions were successfully masked, so that in thin-section they can be seen clustering in the core of the fabric and protruding through the unfinished interior surface.
Armstrong Collection, Black Hole, areas D4, E4-5, F4, F7 and depth 5-6 feet.

Plain necked and shouldered jars are difficult to date since versions appear throughout the first millennium BC. By the fifth century BC, the basic rounded body-shape had replaced angular, carinated shapes for both unfinished 'coarse' and burnished 'fine' wares. The splayed base, and flint tempering of this example suggest a date somewhat earlier than the fifth century. Thin-section analysis groups the fabric with that of the carinated bowl, *LP6*, with which it was found.

From the depth and description of the contexts D4-F7 it seems possible that the sherds could once have come from the filling of a later feature which had not been recognised as such by the excavator. The sherd condition is quite good, but most of the vessel is missing and there are comparatively few joining sherds, so that although this vessel suffered a rather less mobile and disturbed phase before final deposition than some of the late prehistoric and Roman sherds, it scarcely proves the presence of a settlement of this date in the immediate area.

Burnished 'fine' wares
LP6   A single rim sherd from an open bowl with a carinated shoulder formed by thickening the wall on the outside. Sandy textured ware with moderate flint temper mainly below 0.2cm. Black core with patchy brown and grey surfaces, burnished outside and smoothed inside.
Armstrong Collection, Black Hole, D4, depth 4 feet.
The vessel form resembles those of a series of bowls from Pit 1, Darmsden, Suffolk (Cunliffe, 1968: fig. 2, 15-9), and Chinnor, Oxfordshire (Richardson and Young 1951: fig. 5, 49-50).

LP7   More than 20 rim, base and body sherds from a round-bodied bowl, with a raised bead-rim and a flat base. Sandy textured ware, heavily tempered with flint less than 0.2cm in length; black core with variegated brown surfaces. A particularly thin-walled and well-shaped vessel with a glossy burnished finish inside and out.

Armstrong Collection, Black Hole, D4-F5, depth 4-6 feet.

Since it is in the same condition as *LP5*, and was found in the same area and at the same depths, it is reasonable to assume that they were contemporary discards.

Bead-rimmed vessels are normally associated with the period after the third century BC, rather than before. There is, however, a very similar bowl from Site II at West Harling, Norfolk (Clark & Fell 1953: fig. 15, 65) and a number of vessels from Runnymede Bridge (Longley 1980: fig. 37, 421-7) which may indicate a rather earlier date in the first millennium BC. For comments on the context and implications see *LP5* above.

LP8 Two joining sherds from a wide-bodied jar with a narrow everted rim. Dark grey sandy textured ware, with moderate flint tempering mainly below 0.2cm in length. Both the inner and outer surfaces have a good horizontally burnished finish.
Norwich Museum Collection. Floor 42A

Probably to be dated to the Middle Iron Age, as the shape is similar to Little Waltham Form 4 or 5 (Drury 1978). To superficial examination the fabric appears identical to *LP9*, so that it can also be grouped with *LP2 & LP7*. Such an association could be taken to imply a rather earlier date than the third century BC although there is as yet no supporting typological evidence.

LP9 More than 20 sherds from the rim and upper body from one part of the circuit of a plain necked and shouldered bowl. Black ware, heavily tempered with flint mainly less than 0.3cm in length. Due to weathering, no inner surface finish survives and the grits are exposed, but the outer surface retains some of its original smooth burnished finish.
Armstrong Collection. Area S.W. of the Black Hole.

As with *LP8*, the basic shape is difficult to date. It is probably more at home in the Iron Age than the Late Bronze Age, but as with *LP8*, the fabric is very similar to the apparently earlier flint-tempered wares of *LP2* (see p.106).

Grog-tempered ware

A rim sherd from a handmade jar with an upright bead rim. Black sandy textured ware, tempered with black grog and with the occasional large flint chip.

TABLE 13   Inventory of Roman sherds by type and fabric.

SAMIAN

Central Gaul	Drag 31(1): 33(1): 37(1): 45(1) mid-late 2nd century.
East Gaul	Déchelette 64(1): bowl(1) late 2nd century-early 3rd century.

COLOUR-COATED WARES

East Gaul	Roughcast beaker (1)	mid-late 2nd century.
L.N.V.	Bowl, Gillam 342 (1)	late 2nd-4th century.
Unknown	Beakers (2)	3rd-4th century.
Oxfordshire	Bowl (1)	after A.D. 330.

MORTARIA

L.N.V.	(1)	3rd-4th century.
Unknown	(2)	late 2nd-4th century.

AMPHORA

South Spanish	(1)

GLAZED WARES

South-eastern England		(1) late 1st-early 2nd century.

STAMPED-DECORATED WARES

L.N.V./East Anglia		(1) late 1st-late 2nd century.

SAND-TEMPERED WARES

	RIMS	BASES	SHERDS
Dishes	7	7	2
Cheesepress	1	-	-
Jars	12	11	82
'Rustic' Jars	-	-	1
Lid	1	-	-
Total	21	19	85

Roughly finished inner and outer surfaces. Armstrong Collection. Black Hole, no context.

First century BC to mid-first century AD.

Roman and post-Roman sherds

All sherds are small and miscellaneous, none joining, and in a more or less weathered condition which implies they are residual and redeposited. Most are undiagnostic and unclassifiable body sherds, including a few which, to judge from their colour and texture, are more likely to be Medieval rather than Roman in date, and four which are definitely post-Medieval.

The Roman sherds span the period from the first to the late fourth century AD, with a noticeable concentration in the mid- to late-second century. This second century material includes most of the basic types and traded wares normally associated with a flourishing settlement of the period, which, given the absence of any other archaeological evidence of Roman occupation, is somewhat surprising.

Given the poor condition of the sherds and their lack of context, quantification was possible only by a sherd count of fabrics which is given in Table 13. As with the late Prehistoric Pottery, the most notable result is the shortage of rims and bases. Rims give a minimum vessel count of 21, and bases, 19, yet the 85 body sherds are such a miscellaneous collection that each probably represents a different pot.

The imported wares totalling 17 different vessels, include plain and decorated samian from both Central and East Gaul, a roughcast colour-coated beaker from East Gaul and a South Spanish olive oil amphora. The specialised traded wares include colour-coated bowls and mortaria from the Oxfordshire and Lower Nene Valley (L.N.V.) potteries, a small brown glazed beaker from an unknown source in South-eastern England (Arthur 1978: p.278-308) and a stamp-decorated bowl probably from a source in East Anglia (Rodwell 1978: Group 4, p.248-58).

The most unlikely addition to the list of traded wares in the rim sherd from a lug-handled pitcher, Gillam type 40, in sand-tempered grey ware. The type emerged in the early Roman period in Yorkshire, Humberside and Lincolnshire, and was made at a number of different potteries until the end of the Roman period. Early examples were made at Roxby and Dragonby, S. Humberside (Stead 1976: fig. 64, 6; 67, 38-9), later versions at Messingham, S.

Humberside (*ibid*: 71, 13-4), Cantley, S. Yorkshire (Buckland *et al* 1980: fig. 4, 25) Throlam and Crambeck, N. Yorkshire (Corder 1930: fig. 14; 1928: pl. IV, 80-5). The form and fabric of the pitcher suggest Crambeck as the likely source and a date after AD 330 for its manufacture.

The remaining sand-tempered sherds, presumably from local sources, are, with a single exception, undistinguished and limited in range to standard lid, dish and jar types. The exception is a sherd with nodular rustic decoration (74: L 427). Rustic decoration is particularly common in late first, second and early third century contexts in northern Britain, with production centres at Roxby (*ibid*: fig. 66, 22-8), Cantley (*ibid*: 4, 25) and North Hykham Lincolnshire (Thompson 1958: pl. vi, c). However, the distribution spreads thickly into the Midlands and extends into East Anglia, and it has been suggested that there were conservative production centres in the latter area which began in the third century (*ibid*: fig. 6, p. 32-4). The source of this tiny sherd is uncertain; the vessel may have been traded into the area from some workshop to the north-west, or it may be from a more local source. It was probably made in the second century.

There is one sherd from a wheel-made shell tempered jar which is probably late Roman rather than Medieval in date (73: L 164).

Roman sherds in the 'Black Hole' and Shaft X

Nine Roman sherds were apparently recovered in topsoil lying above the Black Hole, they are marked with the depths 2 and 3 (feet). There is a rim sherd from an East Gaulish cup, which dates to the late second or early third centuries. The remaining sherds are sand-tempered grey wares which probably date to the third century AD.

One sherd (76: L 1585), which probably dates to the third or fourth century, was found in Layer 8 of Shaft X. Judging from its size, condition and position in the feature it is unreliable dating evidence, while it may give a *terminus post quem* for its own layer and those above, it could have been intruded by natural agencies, particularly mammalian action. The remaining Roman sherds were found in layers above Layer 8 which are best interpreted as topsoil.

LP11

Three joining sherds from a jar with an upright bead rim. Dark grey ware with burnt patches of re-oxidation on the lower body and sooty patches at the rim; heavily tempered with coarse fossil shell; smoothed-off inner surface, roughly tooled outer. Armstrong Collection, probably upper layers of the Black Hole.

Roman, late-first to mid-second century in date.

Other contexts

Floor 16

1   Rim. Wall-sided mortarium, Gillam 260. Butt ware. Late 2nd-3rd century.

2   Rim. Narrow-necked jar. Micaceous grey ware. Probably 3rd century.

3   Sherd. Jar. Gritty textured grey ware. Possibly Medieval.

Floor 85

1   Rim. 37. Central Gaul. Antonine.

2   Rim. Jar with lid-sealed rim. Gritty textured grey ware. Probably Medieval.

Floor 85a

1   Sherd. Jar. Micaceous grey ware. Possibly 3rd century.

Pit 10

1   Sherd. Jar with double shoulder groove. Micaceous grey ware. Possibly 3rd century.

2   Sherd. From another jar in the same ware.

Pit 11. 3′6″ Black Sand

1   Rim. Flanged dish, Gillam 229. Micaceous grey ware. After c.AD. 275.

2   Rim. Pitcher with countersunk handles. Gillam 40. From the Crambeck potteries. After c.AD 330.

3   Sherd. Necked jar. Gritty textured ware. Probably 3rd or 4th century.

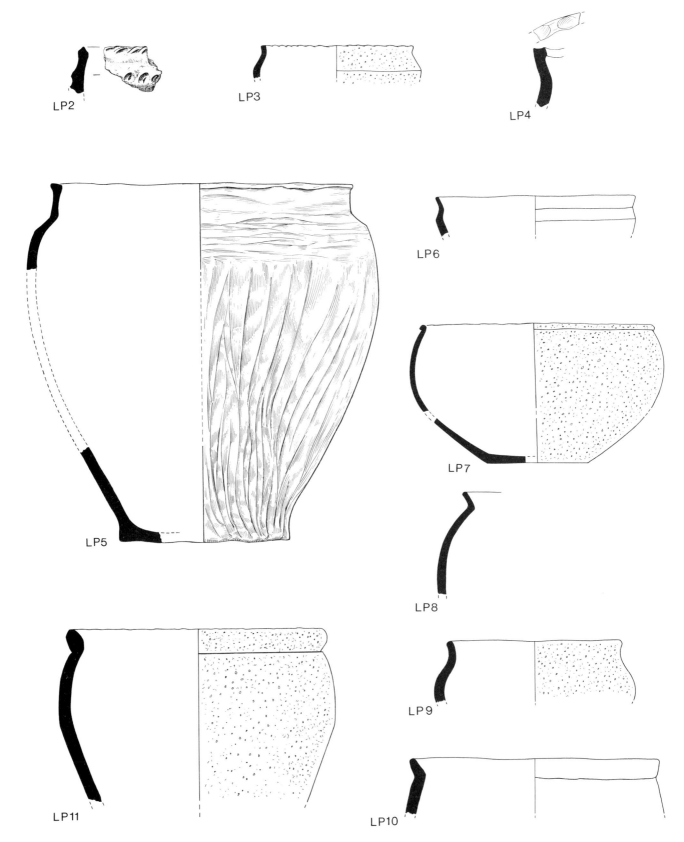

fig. 44   Late Prehistoric, Iron age and Roman Pottery: *LP2*, 1325.5/970.5, Area C;
LP3, β6, 6, Area A; *LP4*, Floor 16; *LP5-7*, Black Hole; *LP8* Floor 42A, *LP9*, Area SW
of the Black Hole; *LP10-11*, Black Hole.

Appendix I

(Identifiable Bronze Age Pottery from East Anglia and Lincolnshire)

	Reference/ Tomalin catalogue	Fabric	Decoration				Horseshoes, arc handles, lugs	Rim				Shoulder Cordon			
			Cord	Comb-point	Linear incised	Rustication		FT top of rim	FT outer rim	FT	Slashed	Plain	FT shoulder	Perforations	Knobs
Biconical Urns															
ESSEX															
Newhouse Farm	E.B1 Couchman 1975						●								
LINCS															
Stainsby	LnB3				●			●		●					
	LnB5	G										●			
	LnB6 ⎰ May 1976	G										●			
	LnB7	G										●			
	LnB8				●										
Metheringham	LnB10 ⎰ Petch 1976	G	●												
	LnB11	G								●					
NORFOLK															
Bircham	N.B1 Butler & Smith 1956						●								
Rockland St Andrew	N.B2	G										●			
Salthouse	N.B3 ⎰ Lawson 1980	G										●			
Needham	N.B4	G					●	●		●		●			
Hockwold	N.B5-8 Tomalin 1983	G	●	●		●	●	●		●		●	●		●
Massingham	N.B9 Tomalin 1983	G	●									●			
Reffley Wood	N.B10 Brailsford 1953	G + Q		●								●			
Bawburgh	N.B11 DeCaux 1942	G										●			
Brettenham	N.B12	G						●		●					
E. Walton	N.B13 ⎰ Lawson 1980	G							●	●					
Bergh Apton	N.B14	F					●			●					
Garboldisham	Sf.B5 Tomalin 1983	G + F					●			●					
NORTHANTS															
Peterborough (Fengate)	Np.B1 Leeds 1922		●												
Burton Latimer	Np.B2 Posnansky 1956	G	●												

	Reference/ Tomalin catalogue	Fabric	Cord	Comb-point	Linear incised	Rustication	Horseshoes, arc handles, lugs	FT top of rim	FT outer rim	FT	Slashed	Plain	FT shoulder	Perforations	Knobs
Biconical Urns															
SUFFOLK															
Hollesley	Sf.B1	G					●			●					
Leiston	Sf.B2 ⎫ Smedley and	G	●				●								
Leiston	Sf.B3 ⎬ Owles 1964	G					●								
Semer	Sf.B4 ⎭	G								●					
Mildenhall Fen	Sf.B6-7 Clark 1936	G	●	●	●	●	●	●	●	●	●	●		●	●
Ardleigh Group and other Bronze Age Pottery															
CAMBS															
Chesterton	VCH Cambs,I, 1938,283					●									
Fordy	Lethbridge 1933														●
Melbourn	Wilkerson 1960											●			
Swaffham - Bulbeck	VCH Cambs,I, 1938,282						●								
Thriplow	Trump 1956											●			
ESSEX															
Ardleigh urnfield	Erith & Longworth 1960	F		●	●	●	●	●	●	●	●	●			
Ardleigh barrows	Couchman 1975	F				●			●	●	●	●		●	●
Barling Hall	Couchman 1977	F				●				●				●	
Bocking	(Colchester Museum)					●									
Braintree	Couchman 1977								●	●				●	
Colchester															
Abbey Field	Abercromby 1912, 469 tris														●
Ackland Ave	(Colchester Museum)					●									
Chitts Hill	Crummy 1977	F + S				●			●	●				●	
Shakespeare Road	(Colchester Museum)					●									
Sheepen Rd	(Colchester Museum)					●									
Dovercourt	Butcher 1923						●								
Fingrinhoe	(Colchester Museum)					●									
Gt Oakley	(Colchester Museum)					●									
Mucking	Inf. M Jones							●	●	●					
Shalford	Benton 1924					●			●	●					
Shoebury	(Colchester Museum)					●		●							
Southchurch	Abercromby 1912, 471									●					
Thurrock	PSA III, 2nd Ser. 406									●					
Walton on Naze				●		●									
White Colne	(Colchester Museum)					●		●							
Witham	VCH Essex, 274					●									
Wix	(Colchester Museum)					●		●							
LINCS															
Billingborough	Chowne 1978	G				●				●	●				
Frieston	Phillips 1933					●				●	●				
Belton	Phillips 1933					●				●					

	References/ Tomalin catalogue	Fabric	Decoration					Rim		Shoulder Cordon				Perforations	Knobs
			Cord	Comb-point	Linear incised	Rustication	Horseshoes, arc handles, lugs	FT top of rim	FT outer rim	FT	Slashed	Plain	FT shoulder		
Ardleigh Group and other Bronze Age Pottery *contd*															
NORFOLK															
Morning Thorpe	Lawson 1980	F + G						●						●	
Snettisham		F								●				●	
Witton OS36										●					
Witton OS93	Lawson 1983												●		
Witton OS200										●			●		
Grimes Graves	this volume	F;Sh;G		●	●	●	●	●	●	●	●	●	●	●	●
NORTHANTS															
Peterborough		voids	●											●	
(Fengate)	Pryor 1980	Sh									●				
SUFFOLK															
Brantham Hall	Gilmour 1976	F;G								●			●	●	
Honington	Fell 1952												●		
Ipswich	(Ipswich Museum)						●								
Kettleburgh 1	O'Connor 1976								●						
Nayland	(Colchester Museum)						●								
Playford	(Ipswich Museum)						●								
Rushmere	(Ipswich Museum)						●								
Sutton Hoo	Longworth & Kinnes 1980							●							
Woodbridge	(Ipswich Museum)						●			●					
Mepal Fen	Fox 1923					●									

Appendix II

(Sites mapped in fig. 19)

A ROW OF PERFORATIONS BELOW RIM

Middle Bronze Age

Sunningdale, Berks	Ellison 1975, pl. 46.
Furzy, Latch Farm, Christchurch, Hants	Calkin 1964, fig. 12, 6.
Ashford, Middlesex	Barrett 1973, fig. 2, 22.
Itford Hill barrow, Beddingham, Sussex	Holden 1972, fig. 9, 16.
Park Brow, Sussex	Wolseley, Smith & Hawley 1927, fig. 1.
Plumpton Plain Site A Sussex.	Hawkes 1935, fig. 1,d.

Late Bronze Age

Stoneyfield-Snailslynch, Farnham, Surrey	Oakley, Rankine & Lowther 1939, Fig. 70.

B DECORATION (USUALLY FINGER-TIP IMPRESSIONS) ON TOP OF RIM

Middle Bronze Age

Brimpton, Berks	S. Lobb, forthcoming.
Knights Farm site 3	Bradley, Lobb, Richards & Robinson 1980, fig. 32, 46.
Sunningdale, Berks	Ellison 1975, pl. 46.
Poundbury, Dorset	Smith in Green, 1987.
Yateley, Hants (Hillfield House)	Piggott 1928, H1.
Kimpton, Hants (E2, E3)	Dacre & Ellison 1981, figs. 18 and 19.
Deal, Kent	Stebbing 1937, fig. 1.
Milton Regis, Kent	Cook 1935; Ellison 1975, pl. 64, 2.
Ramsgate, Kent	Hawkes 1942, fig. 1.
Long Wittenham, Oxon	Case et al 1964/5, fig. 28, 4.
Hanborough, Oxon	Case et al 1964/5, fig. 31.

Stoneyfield-Snailslynch, Farnham, Surrey	Oakley *et al* 1939, fig. 70.
Weybridge, Surrey	Ellison 1975, pl. 60.
Westfield, Woking, Surrey	Ellison 1975, pl.61.

Late Bronze Age

Aldermaston, Berks	Bradley *et al* 1980, 270.
Sulham, Berks	Ellison 1975, pl. 45, 4.
Ivinghoe Beacon, Bucks	Waugh 1968, fig. 19, 99-102.
Puddlehill, Bucks	Inf. C. Saunders.
Kimpton, Hants. (G6)	Dacre & Ellison 1981, fig. 22.
Sturry, Kent	Inf. S. Needham.
Carshalton, Surrey	Inf. L Adkins.
Weston Wood, Surrey	Inf. S Needham.
Green Lane, Farnham	Elsdon, 1982.
Bishopstone, Sussex	Bell 1977, fig. 22, 9 and 11.
New Barn Down, Sussex	Curwen 1934, fig. 17.
Castle Hill, Newhaven, Sussex	Hawkes 1939, figs. 1-2.

C PLAIN SHOULDER CORDON

Middle Bronze Age

Sulham, Berks	Ellison 1975, pl. 45, 7.
Chalton, Hants	Cunliffe 1970, fig. 4, 5.
Deal, Kent	Stebbing 1937, fig. 1.
Hammersmith, London	Ellison 1975, pl. 56, 2.
Long Wittenham, Oxon	Case *et al* 1964/5, fig. 29, 1 and 2.
Standlake, Oxon	Riley 1946/7, pl. III, E.
Itford Hill, Sussex	Burstow & Holleyman 1957, fig. 20.

D KNOBBED CUPS

Middle Bronze Age

Grovelands, Reading, Berks	Ellison 1975, pl 39.
Sulham, Berks	Ellison 1975, pl 42.
Shefford, Berks	Ellison 1975, pl 37.
Knighton Heath, Hampreston Dorset	Petersen 1981, fig. 23, 15 and 33.
Dewlish G1, Dorset	Abercromby 1912, 456k.
Hilton G 2a (Cheselbourne), Dorset	Abercromby 1912, 443.
Horton, Dorset	Dorchester Museum.
Piddlehinton G4, Dorset	Abercromby 1912, 441.
Portland G1 (Sugden), Dorset	Abercromby 1912, 437a.
Poxwell G2b, Dorset	Ellison 1975, pl. 105.
Wimborne, Dorset	Field 1966.
Broughton, Hants.	Abercromby 1912, 253.

Dummer, Hants.	Ellison 1975, pl. 37.
Ightham, Kent	Jessup 1930, fig. 14.
Abingdon, Oxon.	Inf. R. Henderson.
Long Wittenham, Oxon	Case *et al.* 1964/5, fig. 28, 5 and 7.
Stanton Harcourt, Oxon	Hamlin and Case 1963, fig. 10.
Wandsworth, London	Ellison 1975, pl. 58.
Stoneyfield-Snailslynch, Farnham, Surrey	Oakley *et al* 1939, pl. XVIII, 1; Ellison 1975, pl. 57.
Hampton Court, Surrey	Ellison 1975, pl. 57.
Haywards Heath, Sussex	Musson 1954, no. 406.
Swindon, Wilts. (3 examples)	Piggott 1939, fig. 3.

Late Bronze Age

Kimpton, Hants, (E1, G7)	Dacre and Ellison 1981, figs. 19 and 22.
Kingston Hill, Surrey	Kingston Museum.

Appendix III

(Sources of data employed in fig. 21 and 22)

East Anglia

Ardleigh urnfield, Essex	Erith & Longworth 1960
Ardleigh barrows, Essex	Couchman 1975
Brantham Hall, Suffolk	Gilmour 1976
Chitts Hill, Essex	Crummy 1977
Witton, Norfolk	Lawson 1983
Grimes Graves, Norfolk	this volume.

Southern England

Barnes, Isle of Wight	Dunning 1931
Thorny Down, Wiltshire	unpublished study by author; material in Salisbury Museum
Kimpton, Hants	Dacre & Ellison 1981
Sulham, Berks	
Plush, Piddletrenthide, Dorset	Ellison 1975
Deverel Barrow, Dorset	
Knighton Heath, Dorset	Petersen 1981

General

South Eastern Style Collared Urns	Longworth 1984, fig. 33
Food Vessels (Hockwold)	Tomalin 1983, fig. 13
Wessex Biconical Urns in East Anglia	from corpus in Tomalin 1983

References

Abercromby, J., 1912, *The Bronze Age Pottery of Great Britain and Ireland*. 2 vols. (London).

Armstrong, A.L., 1921, 'Flint-Crust engravings, and associated implements, from Grimes Graves, Norfolk'. *Proc. Prehist. Soc. East Anglia*, III, pt III, 434-443.

Armstrong, A.L., 1922, 'Further discoveries of engraved flint-crust and associated implements at Grimes Graves'. *Proc. Prehist. Soc. East Anglia*, III, pt IV, 548-58.

Armstrong, A.L., 1924a, 'Discovery of a new phase of early flint mining at Grimes Graves, Norfolk'. *Proc. Prehist. Soc. East Anglia* IV, pt I, 113-125.

Armstrong, A.L., 1924b, (1) 'Further researches in the primitive Flint Mining area. (2) Discovery of an Early Iron Age site, of Hallstatt Culture'. *Proc. Prehist. Soc. East Anglia* IV, pt II, 182-193.

Armstrong, A.L., 1924c, 'Further excavations upon the engraving floor (floor 85), Grimes Graves'. *Proc. Prehist. Soc. East Anglia*, IV, pt II, 194-202.

Armstrong, A.L. 1927, 'The Grimes Graves problem in the light of recent researches'. *Proc. Prehist. Soc. East Anglia*, V, pt II, 91-136.

Armstrong, A.L., 1932, 'The Percy Sladen Trust Excavations, Grimes Graves, Norfolk. Interim Report 1927-1932'. *Proc. Prehist. Soc. East Anglia*, VII, pt I, 57-61.

Armstrong, A.L., 1934, Grimes Graves, Norfolk. Report on the excavation of Pit 12. *Proc. Prehist. Soc. East Anglia*, VII, pt III, 382-394.

Arthur, P., 1978, 'The lead glazed wares of Roman Britain' in Arthur, P., & Marsh, G., (eds.) *Early Fine Wares in Roman Britain*, BAR 57, 293-356.

Bamford, H.M., 1982, 'Beaker Domestic Sites in the Fen Edge and East Anglia' *East Anglian Arch.* Report No. 16.

Barrett, J., 1973, 'Four Bronze Age Cremation Cemeteries from Middlesex'. *Trans. London and Middlesex Arch. Soc.*, 24, 111-134.

Barrett, J.C., 1980, 'The Pottery of the Later Bronze Age in Lowland England', *Proc. Prehist. Soc.*, 46, 297-319.

Bell, M., 1977, 'Excavations at Bishopstone'. *Sussex Arch. Colls.*, Vol. 115.

Benton, G.M., 1924, 'Cinerary urns of the late Bronze Age discovered at Shalford, Essex'. *Ant. J.*, IV, 265-7.

Bradley, R., Lobb, S., Richards, J. and Robinson, M., 1980, 'Two late Bronze Age settlements on the Kennet gravels: excavations at Aldermaston Wharf and Knight's Farm, Burghfield, Berkshire', *Proc. Prehist. Soc.*, 46, 217-296.

Brailsford, J.W., 1953. *British Museum Guide to Later Prehistoric Antiquities*. (London).

Brewster, T.C.M., 1963, *The Excavation at Staple Howe*.

Buckland, P.C., Magilton, J.R., and Dolby, M.J., 1980, 'The Roman potteries of South Yorkshire: A review'. *Britannia*, 11, 145-226.

Burleigh, R., Hewson, A., Meeks, N., Sieveking, G. & Longworth, I., 1979, 'British Museum Natural Radiocarbon Measurements X', *Radiocarbon*, 21, No. 1, 41-47.

Burstow, G.P. & Holleyman, G.A., 1957, 'Late Bronze Age Settlement on Itford Hill, Sussex', *Proc. Prehist. Soc.*, XXIII, 167-212.

Butcher, C.H., 1923, 'Essex Bronze Implements and Weapons in the Colchester Museum', *Trans. Essex Arch. Soc.*, XVI, 258-267.

Butler, J.J. & Smith, I.F., 1956, 'Razors, Urns and the British Middle Bronze Age', *Univ. London Inst. Arch. Annual. Report*, 12, 20-52.

Calkin, J.B., 1964, 'The Bournemouth Area in the Middle and Late Bronze Age, with the 'Deverel-Rimbury' Problem Reconsidered', *Arch. J.*, CXIX, 1-65.

Case, H.J. *et al*, 1964/5, 'Excavations at City Farm, Hanborough, Oxon, *Oxoniensia*, XXIX-XXX, 1-98.

Chowne, P., 1978, 'Billingborough Bronze Age Settlement: An Interim Note', *Lincs. History and Archaeology*, Vol. 3, 15-21.

Clark, J.G.D., 1936, 'Report on a Late Bronze Age Site in Mildenhall Fen, West Suffolk', *Ant. J.*, XVI, 29-50.

Clark, J.G.D., & Fell, C.I., 1953, 'The Early Iron Age site at Micklemoor Hill, West Harling, Norfolk, and its Pottery'. *Proc. Prehist. Soc.*, XIX, 1-39.

Clarke, D.L., 1970, *Beaker Pottery of Great Britain and Ireland*. 2 vols. (Cambridge).

Clarke, W.G., (ed.), 1915, *Report on the Excavations at Grime's Graves, Weeting, Norfolk, March-May 1914.*

Cook, N., 1935, 'Reports of Local Secretaries', *Arch. Cant.*, XLVII, 239-40.

Corder, P., 1928, *The Roman Pottery at Crambeck, Castle Howard.*

Corder, P., 1930, *The Roman Pottery at Throlam, Holme-on-Spalding Moor, East Yorkshire.*

Couchman, C.R., 1975, 'The Bronze Age Cemetery at Ardleigh, Essex: A Further Consideration', *Essex Archaeology and History* 7, 14-32.

Couchman, C. (Ed.), 1977, 'Work of Essex County Council Archaeology Section 1977', *Essex Arch & History*, 9, 60-94.

Crummy, P., 1977, 'A Bronze Age Cemetery at Chitts Hill, Colchester, Essex'. *Essex Arch. & Hist.* 9, 1-16.

Cunliffe, B., 1968, 'Early pre-Roman Iron Age Communities in Eastern England', *Ant. J.*, 48, 175-91.

Cunliffe, B.W., 1970, 'A Bronze Age settlement at Chalton, Hants', *Ant. J.*, 50, 1-13.

Cunliffe, B.W., 1974, *Iron Age Communities in Britain.* (London).

Curwen, E.C., 1934, 'A Late Bronze Age Farm and a Neolithic pit dwelling on New Barn Down, near Worthing', *Sussex Arch. Colls.*, LXXV, 137-70.

Dacre, M. & Ellison, A.B., 1981, 'A Bronze Age Urn Cemetery at Kimpton, Hampshire', *Proc. Prehist. Soc.*, 47, 147-203.

De Caux, H., 1942, 'A prehistoric site in the Yare Valley', *Norfolk Arch.*, 28(1), 71-5.

Drury, P., 1978, *Excavations at Little Waltham 1970-1971,* CBA Res. Rep. 26.

Dunning, G.C., 1931, 'A Late Bronze Age Urnfield at Barnes, Isle of Wight', *Proc. Isle of Wight Nat. Hist., & Ant. Soc.*, II, Pt. II, 108-117.

Ellison, A.B., 1975, *Pottery and Settlements of the Later Bronze Age in Southern England.* Ph D. Thesis. Univ. of Cambridge.

Ellison, A.B., 1981, 'Towards a Socioeconomic Model for the Middle Bronze Age in Southern England', in Hodder, I., Isaac, G. & Hammond, N. (eds.), *Pattern of the Past; Studies in Honour of David Clarke.* (Cambridge), 413-438.

Ellison, A.B., 1982, 'Middle Bronze Age Pottery', in Drewett, P. 'Later Bronze Age Downland Economy and Excavations at Black Patch, East Sussex', *Proc. Prehist. Soc.*, 48, 361-368.

Elsdon, S., 1982, 'Later Bronze Age Pottery from Farnham, a reappraisal', *Surrey Arch. Colls.*, 73, 127-139.

Erith, F.H. & Longworth, I.H., 1960, 'A Bronze Age Urnfield on Vinces Farm, Ardleigh, Essex', *Proc. Prehist. Soc.*, XXVI, 178-192.

Fell, C.I., 1952, 'A Late Bronze Age Urnfield and Grooved-Ware Occupation at Honington, Suffolk', *Proc. Camb. Arch. Soc.*, XLV, 30-43.

Field, N.H., 1966, 'A Bronze Age Burial Urn from Willett Road, near Wimborne', *Proc. Dorset. Nat. Hist. & Arch. Soc.*, 88, 105-6.

Fox, C. 1923, '*Archaeology of the Cambridge Region*'.

Gardiner, J. 1987 'Late Neolithic and Bronze Age Pottery', in B. Cunliffe *Hengistbury Head Dorset I: The Prehistoric and Roman Settlement, 3500 BC-AD 500*, Sect. 2.4, 38-47.

Gibson, A.M., 1982, *Beaker Domestic Sites. A study of the domestic pottery of the late third and early second millennia B.C. in the British Isles.* BAR 107.

Gilmour, R.A., 1976, 'Beaker and Bronze Age Burials at Brantham Hall', *Proc. Suffolk Inst. of Arch.* 33, 116-130.

Green, C.J.S., 1987, 'Excavations at Poundbury, Dorchester, Dorset, Vol. I: The Settlements. *Dorset Nat. Hist. & Arch. Soc.*, Monograph.

Hamlin, A. & Case, H.J., 1963. 'Excavation of Ring-Ditches and other Sites at Stanton Harcourt'. (Hamlin). 'Notes on the Finds and on Ring-Ditches in the Oxford Region' (Case). *Oxoniensia*, XXVIII, 1-52.

Hawkes, C.F.C., 1935, 'The Pottery from the sites on Plumpton Plain', *Proc. Prehist. Soc.*, I, 39-49.

Hawkes, C.F.C., 1939, 'The Pottery from Castle Hill, Newhaven', *Sussex Arch. Colls.*, LXXX, 269-292.

Hawkes, C.F.C, 1942, 'The Deverel Urn and the Picardy Pin: A Phase of Bronze Age Settlement in Kent', *Proc. Prehist. Soc.*, VIII. 26-47.

Hedges, J. & Buckley, D., 1978, 'Excavations at a Neolithic Causewayed Enclosure, Orsett, Essex, 1975', *Proc. Prehist. Soc.*, 44, 219-308.

Holden, E.W., 1972, 'A Bronze Age Cemetery-Barrow on Itford Hill, Beddingham, Sussex', *Sussex Arch. Colls.* CX, 70-117.

Ince, A.G., 1928, 'Pedestal Urns in Kent', *Ant. J.*, 8, 93-4.

Jessup, R.F., 1930, *The Archaeology of Kent.*

Jones, M.U., & Bond, D., 1980. 'Late Bronze Age settlement at Mucking, Essex', in Barrett, J. & Bradley, R.J. (eds.), *Settlement and Society in the British Later Bronze Age.* BAR. No. 83.

Kendall, Rev. H.G.O., 1925, 'Arrowheads at Grimes's Graves'. *Proc. Prehist. Soc. East Anglia*, V, pt I, 64-6.

Lawson, A.J., 1980, 'The Evidence for Later Bronze Age Settlement and Burial in Norfolk', in Barrett, J. & Bradley, R.J. (eds.) *Settlement and Society in the British Later Bronze Age.* BAR. No. 83.

Lawson, A.J., 1983, 'The Archaeology of Witton, near North Walsham, Norfolk', *East Anglian Arch.*, 18.

Leeds, E.T., 1922, 'Further Discoveries of the Neolithic and Bronze Ages at Peterborough', *Ant. J.*, 2, 220-237.

Legge, A.J. 1981, The Agricultural Economy in Mercer, R.J. - *Grimes Graves, Norfolk. Excavations* 1971-72: Vol. 1. DOE Arch. Rep. No. 11.

Legge, A.J., forthcoming. Grimes Graves fascicule.

Lethbridge, T.C. 1933, 'Investigation of the Ancient Causeway in the Fen between Fordy and Little Thetford, Cambs', *Proc. Camb. Ant. Soc.*, XXXV, 86-9.

Longley, D., 1980, 'Runnymede Bridge 1976: Excavations on the site of a Later Bronze Age Settlement'. *Surrey Arch. Soc. Res.* Vol. 6.

Longworth, I.H., 1971, 'The Pottery' in Wainwright, G.J., *et al*, 'The Excavation of a Late Neolithic Enclosure at Marden, Wiltshire'. *Ant. J.*, LI, 197-215.

Longworth, I.H., 1979, 'The Neolithic and Bronze Age Pottery' in Wainwright, G.J., *Mount Pleasant, Dorset: Excavations 1970-1971*. Soc. of Ant. of London Res. Rep. XXXVII.

Longworth, I.H., 1981, 'Neolithic and Bronze Age Pottery' in Mercer, R.J., *Grimes Graves, Norfolk. Excavations 1971-72 Vol. 1*. DoE Arch. Rep. No. 11.

Longworth, I.H. 1984 *'Collared Urns of the Bronze Age in Great Britain and Ireland'*.

Longworth, I.H. & Kinnes, I.A., 1980, *Sutton Hoo Excavations 1966, 1968-70*. BM Occasional Paper. No. 23.

Manby, T.G., 1974, *Grooved Ware Sites in Yorkshire and the North of England*. BAR 9.

Manby, T.G., 1980, 'Neolithic and Bronze Age Pottery' in Wheeler, H., 'Excavation at Willington, Derbyshire, 1970-1972. *Derbys. Arch. J.*, XCIX, 146-162.

Matthews, C.L., 1976 *Occupation Sites on a Chiltern Ridge. Excavations at Puddlehill and Sites near Dunstable, Bedfordshire. Pt I Neolithic, Bronze Age and Early Iron Age*. BAR 29.

May, J., 1976, *Prehistoric Lincolnshire: History of Lincolnshire 1*.

Mercer, R.J. 1981, *Grimes Graves, Norfolk: Excavations 1971-72: Vol. 1*. DOE Arch. Rep. No. 11.

Musson, R.C., 1954 'An Illustrated Catalogue of Sussex Beaker and Bronze Age Pottery', *Sussex Arch. Colls.*, 92, 106-124.

Oakley, K.P., Rankine, W.F. & Lowther, A.W.G. 1939, *A Survey of the Prehistory of the Farnham District (Surrey)*, Surrey Arch. Colls.

O'Conner, B., 1976, 'Two Groups of Prehistoric Pottery from Kettleburgh' *Proc. Suffolk Inst. of Arch.*, XXXIII, 231-240.

Peake, A.E., 1916, 'Recent Excavations at Grime's Graves' *Proc. Prehist. Soc. East Anglia*, II, pt. II, 268-319.

Peake, A.E., 1917, Further Excavations at Grime's Graves. *Proc. Prehist. Soc. East Anglia*, II. pt. III, 409-436.

Peake, A.E., Excavations at Grimes Graves During 1917. *Proc. Prehist. Soc. East Anglia*, III, pt. I, 73-93.

Petch, D.F., 1961, 'Archaeological Notes for 1959 and 1960', *Lincs. Architect. & Archaeol. Soc. Rep. & Papers*, 9, 1-25.

Petersen, F.F., 1981. *'The Excavation of a Bronze Age Cemetery on Knighton Heath Dorset'*, BAR British Series 98.

Phillips, C.W., 1933, 'The present state of Archaeology in Lincolnshire. VII and VIII', *Arch. J.*, XC, 132-146.

Piggott, S., 1928, 'Bronze Age and Late Celtic Burials from Yateley, Hants'. *Berks. Arch. J.*, 32, No. 2, 69-73.

Piggott, C.M., 1939, 'Late Bronze Age Urns from Swindon', *Wilts. Arch. Mag.*, XLVIII, 353-56.

Posnansky, M., 1956, *Some considerations of the Pleistocene Chronology and prehistory of parts of the East Midlands*. PhD thesis. University of Nottingham.

Potter, T.W.J., 1976, 'Excavations at Stonea, Cambs: Sites of the Neolithic, Bronze Age and Roman Periods', *Proc. Camb. Ant. Soc.*, 66, 23-54.

Pryor, F., 1974, *Excavation at Fengate, Peterborough, England: The First Report*. Royal Ontario Museum. Arch. Mono. 3.

Pryor, F., 1980. *Excavation at Fengate, Peterborough, England. The Third Report*. Northants. Arch. Soc. Mono. 1.

Richardson, K.M. & Young, A., 1951. 'An Iron Age A site on the Chilterns', *Ant. J.*, 31, 132-48.

Riley, D.N., 1946/7, 'A Late Bronze Age and Iron Age site on Standlake Downs, Oxon'. *Oxoniensia*, XI/XII, 27-43.

Rodwell, W., 1978, 'Stamp decorated pottery of the early Roman Period in Eastern England' in Arthur, P. & Marsh, G., (eds.) *Early fine wares in Roman Britain*. BAR 57, 225-292.

Smedley, N. & Owles E., 1964, 'Pottery of the Early and Middle Bronze Age in Suffolk', *Proc. Suffolk Inst. Arch.*, XXIX, 174-197.

Smith, I.F., 1985, 'The Pottery' in Shennan S.J., Healy F. and Smith I.F. 'The Excavation of a Ring-Ditch at Tye Field, Lawford, Essex.' *Arch. J.*, 142, 150-215.

Smith, R.A., 1915, 'Pottery, Worked Bones and Worked Chalk' in Clarke, W.G. (ed.) *'Report on the Excavations at Grimes's Graves, Weeting, Norfolk, March-May 1914*, 208-217.

Stead, I.M., 1976, *Excavations at Winterton Roman Villa*. DOE Arch. Rep. 9.

Stebbing, W.P.D. 1937, 'Bucket Urns found near Deal'. *Ant. J.*, XVII, No. 1., 73.

Thompson, F.H. 1958, 'A Romano-British pottery Kiln at North Hykeham, Lincolnshire'. *Ant. J.*, 38, 15-51.

Tomalin, D.J., 1983, *British Biconical Urns: their Character and Chronology and their relationship with indigenous Early Bronze Age ceramics*. PhD. thesis. Univ. of Southampton.

Trump, D.H., 1956, 'The Bronze Age Barrow and Iron Age Settlement at Thriplow', *Proc. Cam. Ant. Soc.*, XLIX, 1-12.

Waugh, H., 1968, 'The Pottery' (from Ivinghoe), *Records of Bucks.*, XVIII. Pt 3, 219-234.

White, D.A., 1982, 'The Bronze Age Cremation Cemeteries at Simons Ground, Dorset'. *Dorset Nat. Hist. & Arch. Soc.*, Mono. 3.

Wilkerson, J.C., 1960, 'Bronze Age Barrows at Melbourn', *Proc. Cam. Ant. Soc.*, LIII, 55-57.

Wolseley, G.R., Smith, R.A. & Hawley, W., 1927, 'Prehistoric and Roman Settlements on Park Brow', *Archaeologia*, LXXVI, 1-40.